Bedtime Stories for Adults

Depression and Anxiety. Have a Peaceful, Relaxing Sleep and Wake up Fresh, Happy, & Without Worries. Calm Your Mind NOW

document, including, but not limited to, — errors, omissions, or inaccuracies.

Table of Contents

Introduction

If you've found yourself lying in bed often without being able to fall asleep, or you find yourself struggling to stay asleep, you may suffer from insomnia. Insomnia is one of those problems that could be isolated on its own, or it could be something that is indicative that you have other problems that need to be addressed. If you find that it is hard for you to fall asleep, stay asleep, or get back to sleep, you may need to address this sleep disorder, especially if it starts to impact your own personal quality of life. It can harm your energy level or your mood, as well as your efficiency and health. While we all need slightly different amounts of sleep, most adults require between seven and eight hours nightly, and if you are not getting at least that, you may be struggling with insomnia.

If you are, you are not alone by any means—most adults suffer from what is known as an acute episode of insomnia, where for a few days or weeks, there is a struggle sleeping, typically tied to trauma or stress. However, some people have longer-lasting chronic insomnia that can last for months at a time. If your sleep is suffering, know that you don't have to put up with it. You can make some very simple changes to your life to fix the problem.

In this book, we are going to be addressing two common causes of insomnia—anxiety and depression. Both of these can lead to major problems with feelings of insomnia, but you can learn to cope with them. Through learning how to navigate your own life and how you choose to interact with yourself, you can start to alleviate that anxiety and depression, and as those symptoms alleviate, your sleep should improve dramatically. This is because anxiety and depression are both known to negatively impact sleep one way or another.

You cannot "cure" depression or anxiety through meditative techniques—the anxiety and depression will still be there, but you will also be able to approach the situation better as well. You are learning to cope with the negative feelings that otherwise would have controlled you and prevented you from allowing the anxiety and depression to keep your mind reeling all night long. When you have the ability to cope with the negative thoughts that will typically get in your way, you realize that you are far more capable of succeeding at coping with your feelings than you were before. As a result, you should see some alleviation of insomnia.

This book is designed to help you to cope with your anxiety and depression through mindful bedtime stories. These are stories that require you to quietly focus on what is written, listening, and surrendering yourself to what you want to hear. As a result, you will be able to cope better. In this book, it is assumed that you have some degree of mindfulness background. This book is the third in a series of meditative stories meant to aid in the alleviation of anxiety and depression to aid in sleeping better, and it will use techniques that have been taught throughout the previous two as well.

The first book introduced you to the concept of mindfulness—it worked to teach you gentle mindful meditation through the use of mindful breathing, body scans, and affirmations. Each of these three techniques worked to help alleviate those stressors to allow for sleep to occur.

The second book expanded upon those basic techniques, introducing progressive relaxation. Progressive relaxation builds upon body scans, allowing you to begin to work better to help yourself with consciously relaxing several parts of your body little by little until you are done. If you can do this, you will realize that you actually do have the power to calm yourself down over time, something that is highly beneficial to just about anyone.

Finally, this book will introduce you to the use of passive thought observation without judgment for the moment that you are in. As you go through the use of passive thought observation, you learn how to keep yourself at the moment, aware of what is happening within your mind, but you do not engage with the thoughts that you have. You simply let them pass as they are without complaint and without judgment. This helps you to learn where your mind stands so you can be certain that you know what is causing the feelings that you have. Usually, the feelings are caused by certain types of thoughts that then trigger them.

When you can find the cause of the feelings, you can then address them in your life. If through passive observation, you realize that your biggest problem is with the fact that ultimately you are caught up in your emotion, you can then address the cause of the emotions to prevent them in the first place. This is where passive thought observation comes into play.

Passive Thought Observation

Passive thought observation works to allow yourself to simply focus on the moment. When you use it, you find yourself simply sitting and becoming aware of your thoughts. You let them pass you, one by one, so that you can begin to see what is going on in your mind. Your thoughts are constantly at work within yourself. They are able to be tracked, one by one, as they pass in your mind. You can see them filling your mind, then drifting away. In doing this, you quietly listen to yourself and watch what happens.

This meditative technique makes you a visitor to your own mind—a quiet observer that is simply watching as the thoughts pass you by. If you want to do this, you must learn to focus your mind, listening to yourself, and then forcing yourself to avoid responding. It builds self-discipline and helps you to ensure that, ultimately, you don't simply become reflexively responsive. Ideally, you would ensure that you are able to respond accordingly and in a way that is beneficial rather than lashing out.

If this is something that you want to practice, the best starting point is with mindful breathing and a body scan to relax, at which point you can shift your focus away so that you can better influence yourself. When you are able to get to that point of mindful awareness, your next step is to make sure that you let your thoughts start to drift, and simply follow them. You may be surprised to see where they take you.

Each story is designed to be a calming slice of life story about the various adventures (and sometimes misadventures) of Sophie Rogers, a young woman that lives in the Pacific Northwest with her German shepherd pal Bella. Together, and sometimes separately, they get out and enjoy their lives, and the stories of her day to day life can help you to relax and soothe yourself into a state in which you will be able to relax. As you read, you should find yourself calming down and preparing for a night of sleep. Each of the options that are provided to you should be fun and engaging without keeping you up at night. They are designed to provide yourself with something that you can focus on so that you can relax as well. They will gently guide you through a wide range of techniques that are meant to slow down your mind and provide a peaceful clarity to yourself. If you listen closely to the meditations, following along with the instructions, you should find yourself beginning to relax while exploring beautiful scenes and discovering techniques that can help you to defeat the anxiety that you feel.

Hopefully, by following along with these stories, you find yourself starting to relax more and more. It is the hope that as you do read, the story will feel immersive enough that you will be able to pay closer attention to what is on the pages in front of you. It is my hope that as you read over this, you will discover that you are actually quite interested in hearing about Sophie and her friends and that the more that you listen to her and with her, the easier it becomes to sleep. Her stories are not meant to keep you awake, nor are they designed to bother you or make you want to go out and do something. They are here so you can properly focus and begin to sleep, little by little. As you use these guided meditations and stories for yourself, hopefully, you start to feel sleepier and sleepier—hopefully, you find yourself desiring time to sleep, and you are actually able to make it happen.

So, are you ready to get started? Are you ready to start exploring the world of meditation and everything that it has to offer you? Let's dive in!

Story 1: Garden of Rainbows

Sophie has always enjoyed gardening as a child, but in her adulthood, she found that she never bothered to do much with it. She didn't have the time or energy, but she has finally committed to designing a beautiful garden. Armed with her trusty gardening tools and plenty of space in need of utilizing, she is ready to turn her back yard into her own personal paradise once and for all, blooming with flowers and buzzing with life.

Sophie yawned as she sipped at her morning coffee with her laptop sitting in front of her. She sat at her dining table, next to the window looking out over her yard. It was a nice-looking little yard but was rather plain. She ran a hand through her dark hair and frowned to herself as she looked out. There wasn't much to catch her eye—the yard was mostly just an expanse of grass for her German shepherd, Bella, to run throughout, and she knew that. It wasn't meant to be glamorous or perfect—it just had to offer her pup a chance to frolic around when Sophie wasn't really feeling walk time. The entire yard was gently sloped downward, and for her, that had always been a bit of a negative. Sure, Bella could run up and down the yard, and sure, she could always get those extra steps in herself as well, but she wasn't particularly fond of the yard. It was boring and bland, and she wished that there was a bit more pizzaz to it. Where were the colors? The nice, eye-catching details? The flowers that would attract hummingbirds and honeybees? She felt her yard was sorely lacking, and it was a point of contention for poor Sophie. She didn't know what to do, but she knew that she needed to do something quickly. She glanced away from her yard to look around.

Her neighbors' yards were filled with either children's toys and the happy squeals of kids running amok or with immaculate landscaping that was so well kept that she was honestly a bit in awe. How did they get their plants to look so perfectly groomed, or to make their flowers as brightly colored? It was amazing to her—she had no idea how they did it, and she wasn't sure that she had the green thumb to make that work for her either. For Sophie, she wanted something easy to look at but also low-maintenance. She just had to figure out what that would be. With a sigh, Sophie turned her attention back to her computer to type away at her work. She was working on an article about the summer push for hydroponic gardening and how great it was, especially when the plants were stacked to make use of the vertical space available to the gardener.

"That's it!" Sophie cried out loud as the sudden revelation hit her—what if *she* were to make it a point to build her own garden? What if *she* were the one going out of her way to tier the garden to enjoy the slopes while still making the most out of the situation? She could transform just one half of the garden into some nice, tiered beds while leaving the other half of the yard free for Bella to enjoy. It seemed like the perfect opportunity and the best of both worlds.

Besides, being able to enjoy the garden and the sights and smells it would bring with it sounded plenty worth it to her at the moment.

Of course, what good is deciding to plan without having something that she could utilize for herself? What good is trying to figure out what she could do if she didn't know the first thing about different plants anyway? Sophie spent the rest of the day typing away at her computer, doing research, taking notes, and planning. When she set her mind to something, it was rare that she actually got sidetracked. She was very much a one-track mind kind of person, and now that she had set her sights on being able to put in a garden herself, she was determined to make it happen. All she had to do was make it a point to go shopping to pick up all the supplies sooner rather than later, and the sooner that she did so, the sooner she would be able to get to work.

She didn't waste any time, either—once her preliminary planning was done, she decided that it was time to go shopping immediately. She already had basic gardening tools present in her yard—rakes, shovels, and the like were all present without her needing to buy new ones. But, what she was lacking was the materials to start building tiered garden walls. She needed concrete, lots of rocks, and the patience to bring it all home on her own. She also needed plenty of flowers and soil as well. With that in mind, she began her shopping trip. It was ambitious, but she was confident that she could make it work on her own. She knew that she had the dive that she would need to ensure that the garden all came together nicely. She just had to set out and make it happen.

Shopping was the easy part, and before she knew it, Sophie was back at home, staring at the giant bags of stone and concrete that she would need to bring in. All she would need to do is make it a point to find a way to get everything in. If she could do that, she knew that she would be just fine. But, everything was far heavier than she had accounted for—she had asked for help when loading up in her car, and now, it was all on her to drag it out, bring it to the back, and get to work.

Rather than worrying about that immediately, Sophie chose to tackle the planning of the space first. She chose to make time to dig out the different spaces that she would be utilizing first. With a hoe in hand, she started marking out along her sod, where she wanted to put in the walls and started tearing down the soil that she would need to move. Clearing the area out was definitely one of the hardest parts of the whole job. She had to clear out some of the space and dig along the tiers that she wanted. Each of her tiers was going to be roughly 2 feet tall with about two feet of gardening space at each tier. She dug carefully, creating three distinct tiers that she would be using for her garden. It would be perfect, she told herself— the garden space was open enough that she could get a wide variety of flowers while also not taking over the whole yard. She was glad to have something breaking up the monotony of it all while still enjoying the space that she had.

The task of digging out the dirt, one shovelful at a time, was far more exhausting than she had expected. She could feel the hot sun beating on her neck, and she could feel the sweat starting to run down her face as well. It was almost overwhelming how hot it felt as she was actively working the land, but with a few well-timed iced tea breaks and plenty of water and perseverance, she was able to finish up digging with just a sore body as the cost.

From there came the time to dig out the concrete. It was time to make sure that the wall would sustain itself. She knew that building the wall up was important—but it also had to be secure. She had been told to choose pre-mixed concrete to use for her wall to make sure that it would be strong enough. Dumping the concrete mixture into a big bucket and mixing it with water, she was ready to start assembling the wall. She had to dump it straight into each footing of her tier to create a nice layer there for support, with rebar pushed in every foot or so along the way. From there, it was time to let everything dry, and Sophie was incredibly grateful for the chance to take a break and relax. She knew that she would need that time to herself and that peace of mind, so she gladly took it.

The next morning, Sophie awoke, tired, grumpy, and sore, but determined to ensure that she had finished everything up. She was determined to ensure that her garden would be finished, however, so she pushed through the discomfort with a groan and a desire to see her final product. After breakfast, a coffee, and a

bit of relaxation time, she was right back out there to
build up her wall.

Next came combining the mortar and using it so she
could begin to build the wall up as well. The wall was
relatively simple to put together, and she found that it
was incredibly easy to simply slather the mortar
between the stones that she was placing into position.
This part went rapidly, and before she knew it, she
had a beautiful wall in light, warm colors. It looked
great, she told herself as she looked at the three
curved tiers that built up half of her yard. She loved
how they looked as they grew across everything.

Another day passed with everything firming up, and
finally, it was time to get to business. Her favorite part
of the process was the part where she got to plant all
of her flowers right into the space that she had
designed, and now that everything was dry, she was
eager to get started. "You ready, Bells?" she asked her
dog as she got ready that third morning to get started.
It was going to be hard work to fill up those beds, she
told herself, but it would be worth it—the view would
be great.

The first step of the day was ensuring that she had
plenty of soil all ready to go and tucked into each of
the tiers. With that done, it was time to start on
everything else, slowly and carefully filling up the
plots of land with flowers. Sophie wanted to be
strategic about things—she wanted to have a beautiful
garden where the colors felt almost like a rainbow as
they bloomed. She was thrilled to realize that she had

plenty of space to do so. Being able to set up all of the flowers in such a nice order would be perfect for her—and all she had to do was get started on building it all up.

Sophie had picked up all sorts of different flowers for her garden. The first tier, she told herself, would have to be red and orange flowers. This gave her plenty of options, and when she had spent the time weighing her options, she settled on red roses and amaryllis flowers right along with that top row, with a few bushels of small, delicate peonies as well. They all played well together, she thought—they were beautiful shades of red and all different heights, which meant that she would have some very real variety in her garden space if she wanted it.

Next came a need for orange flowers to grow in her garden. Orange had actually been somewhat tricky for her to find as she was shopping, she had realized, but ultimately, a few well-picked zinnias did the job, and she scattered them through that first tier near the divider between the first and second. It was beautiful.

Then came yellow flowers, and for that, there was nearly no shortage. Yellow, it turned out, was a pretty popular flower color. Yellow also offered a stunning flash of color to the garden, she had come to realize. Yellow lilies were planted throughout the space, along with a few yellow tulips and rose bushes as well. Altogether, they would create a marvelous splash of yellow across the garden that she would be unable to deny would be beautiful.

From there came a bush of blue hydrangeas all spattered across the garden as well. They would grow into larger flowers, she knew, but they would also create a wondrous effect while they transitioned colors. It would be a wonderful addition to the garden as well, and they were easy to find as well.

Finally, Sophie needed a layer of purple flowers right along the bottom to complete her vision of her beautiful, rainbow layered garden. Violets made the most obvious choice there in that bottom row, and so they were added with ease. They all melded together to create that nice rainbow effect, and Sophie was *in love.*

With the garden all completed and watered, Sophie collapsed against her house, panting and aching. It had been hard work, but it was absolutely essential to ensuring that looking out with morning coffee wasn't miserable. She was looking forward to seeing just how her garden would turn out as it all had the chance to grow into place. And, she couldn't deny it either—she was *proud* of herself. It was not easy to build such a nice garden, nor was it something that she felt she could do on her own. She had to put her own sweat equity into creating that beautiful look, and she was ready to own it. She was certain that she could get plenty of likes and shares if she posted it on social media, and to be frank, she was too excited to wait for too long.

Of course, that would have to wait until after she had a chance to shower and soak in a bathtub to relieve her aching muscles. The prior three days had been exhausting, and while Sophie was happy to do the work, she was also thoroughly drained after having gone through it all. She had no idea just how exhausting it all would be to build it all up, little by little, all as just one person. Everything from moving the items from one place to another to digging the pits and holes and everything else was thoroughly draining.

But, as exhausting as it was, it was also incredibly satisfying as well. It was perhaps one of the most satisfying things that she had done in a long while—being able to say that she had constructed her own tiered garden all by herself was incredibly fulfilling. After all, she proved that she had the skill and the fortitude to do so.

Sophie's bath was perhaps the most enjoyable one that she had had in a very long time. She was thrilled to just soak in the warmth, enjoying every moment of it as long as she could. Every muscle in her body was so grateful for the chance to unwind and to soak up the comfort of the water, and she loved it. She soaked for as long as she could stand—long past her fingers pruning up to and all the way until her water finally lost its heat. When the temperature was no longer pleasant, she hopped out, feeling rejuvenated after her chance to unwind, and she decided to enjoy her first real day of being able to admire her yard at her spot from the coffee table.

It didn't take long until she was right back at her dining table with her laptop and a cup of coffee. She stared out into the yard and smiled to herself, feeling that sense of self-satisfaction as she did so. It was absolutely gorgeous to look out over everything. The flowers, though they had room to bush up and grow more vibrant, looked great where they were. They were all placed carefully between the different tiers, lining up nicely and growing together well. The colors worked well as they faded throughout the rainbow, and she loved the diversity in different types of flowers, all assembled carefully.

Taking a sip of coffee, Sophie had to congratulate herself on a job very well done. She had lacked the confidence she had needed at first, but now that it was done, she had to admit that she had outdone herself. It was gorgeous. And even better, it didn't take up all of the space in her yard either, which was the best part of all. She still had plenty of room for Bella to run around and plenty of room just to enjoy the scenery. As she sat there, looking over everything, she felt at peace and satisfied with herself. She felt proud of the efforts she put into everything and ready to move on in her life. She was ready to tackle the next big project that she would be pursuing, whatever that may have been—so long as it was not another DIY building a structure.

Maybe a tree, she told herself absently as she turned her computer on and took another sip of coffee. A tree wouldn't be nearly as difficult to plant and get started as a big tiered garden... Right?

Story 2: Gone Fishing

It's fishing time! Sophie has never been a big fan of fishing, but her new boyfriend, Felix, has insisted that she gives it a shot with him at least once. Reluctantly willing, she has gone with him to the lake for the day for a nice bonding event. Boats, fishing poles, and a long day alone together... What could go wrong?

Sophie was never much one for hunting or fishing. She didn't like the idea of pulling out an animal and killing them to eat. Sure, she enjoyed eating meat—she could never give up bacon or steak to go the vegetarian route—but that didn't mean that she needed to see where her food came from first-handed! She didn't need to be the one to kill it if she wanted to eat it! She was firmly in the don't ask, don't tell camp when it came to where her food came from, and while some people found that meant she was either weak or hypocritical because she didn't want to see that animals suffered to feed her, she did it because she didn't want to feel bad for the animals. She *knew* that when she was eating a nice steak, it came from a cow, but she tried to distance the two in her mind. Eating fish that she or her family had caught? That, on the other hand, had always been difficult for her. The cow that she was eating was already dead—there was no undoing that. If she didn't buy it, it could end up going to waste. But, with an animal that she would have to harvest herself? That didn't seem as justifiable in her book. She had seen it alive—she couldn't justify ending its life just for herself. But, despite her protests that she gave Felix, he gave her that pouty puppy look that he seemed to master, and she found herself giving in before she knew what was happening. She couldn't tell him no when she saw those pleading, warm brown eyes.

Felix had met Sophie only a month or so prior to their fishing trip. It was going to be one of the last—the weather was already starting to get chillier, and the sun was setting earlier and earlier every day. But, Felix was determined to show her the wonders of fishing, so she decided to give him that one win. "Because you're too cute to let down," she told him fondly when she agreed to give it a shot. She meant it, too. He was *gorgeous*. He was conventionally attractive, and though she was not one that would have turned down a genuinely good guy, she definitely enjoyed the eye candy when she could get it. So, between his good looks, his charm, and her fondness for him, she agreed.

Felix had told her that they needed to get up early— they had to be up before the sun rose up so they could get on the road. The best local place to go fishing, Felix had insisted, was not too far away—but it would take a few hours to get there. It was worth it, though, he had made it a point to tell her. He loved fishing, and he wasn't about to just let the season end without going one last time. Sure, they could go fishing all winter long if they wanted to, but Felix was quick to let her know that he preferred going when he could still feel his fingers after being outside for an hour or two.

Sophie was up first thing in the morning, just as she had agreed to be. She was not very happy about it—but she was. She got up, out of bed, and forced herself to muster up some sort of enthusiasm over everything. Of course, that enthusiasm was kind of hard to manage when she was so tired. The first order of business was definitely making coffee, she told herself, and off she went, down the stairs and to the kitchen, so she could make her drink. She brewed the magical, warm liquid as she meandered around the kitchen, still almost half asleep, with just the light above her stovetop on.

The number on the microwave glowed dimly in the darkness, the neon green lines creating the time: 4:27, according to the steady blinking, and Sophie yawned to herself. She was ready to get back into bed at such an ungodly hour, but she couldn't let Felix down. So, she went about her morning as normally as she could.

Felix was there promptly at 5:13, and Sophie found herself climbing into his pickup truck. It was an older one—one that he wouldn't care so much about if it got muddy or damaged during off-roading, he told her. He normally drove something that was much more fuel-efficient, but if they were going into the mountains, he had told her, they needed to have something that could get through anything, and that beast of a truck could.

The back was loaded up with a bunch of fishing equipment that Sophie couldn't name, she had noted as she climbed up. She had chosen to wear the most outdoorsy clothes she had, hoping she wouldn't find herself running something that she would miss. Eventually, she had settled on a plain black long sleeve shirt with a turtleneck, with a vest over it. She also brought a thick fleece jacket with her for the coldest parts of their trip, and a pair of gloves that she had hoped she wouldn't need. There was also a bag of clothes that she could use if she got wet somehow, and she wore a pair of waterproof hiking boots on her head, with a wool hat pulled over her head. She let her hair hang loosely at the moment, not worried so much about whether it got dirty. It could be washed easily, at least.

"Good morning, beautiful," Felix purred, planting a kiss on her cheek as she buckled herself in.

"Mmm…" she began, only to yawn sleepily, pulling her arms tightly around her. The crisp fall chill still hung in the air, leaving her shivering. She was surprised that it was so cold in the mornings—she was almost never outside at that time. If she was awake at all, she was letting Bella run out to relieve herself. Then it was

right back into the warm embrace of her comfortable
bed.

"Coffee?" he asked, glancing over at her as he pulled
out of her driveway to start their journey. He seemed
perfectly fine being awake at such an hour, and Sophie
sleepily marveled at the way that he seemed totally
fine. She simply nodded her head in response, and he
chuckled. "That, I can do."

They stopped into a drive-thru café to pick up a few
drinks before heading on their way. They drove in
comfortable silence, sipping at coffee as they went.
Sophie watched as the city gave way to suburbs, and
suburbs eventually gave way to the wilderness. They
lived relatively close to mountains, and before long,
they were surrounded by thick, green forest. Most of
the trees were evergreens, so despite the autumn chill
and the occasional blazing orange trees in the
mountains, they were still green. It wasn't called the
Evergreen State for anything, Sophie mused absently
as she watched the trees.

It was dusky outside—the sky was threatening to light
up, but the sun had not yet managed to rise high
enough to be seen over the mountains. Soon, however,
they could see the golden rays of dawn piercing
through the darkness, and the sky grew brighter. They
pulled off of the main road through the mountain to
turn into a small path that Sophie would have never
seen before. In fact, though she had gone through
those mountains before, she had never actually
noticed that it was there in the first place. They drove

deeper into the wooded area, and Sophie found herself feeling grateful that, at the very least, they had sunlight to lighten up space. The woods were dense and wild and seemed like the perfect scene for a wild bear or cougar to walk right past them. At the very least, in the sunlight, they would be able to see everything before it approached them. That made her feel a little bit better, even though she was totally out of her element.

They continued along that little mountain road for a long while, surrounded by trees that created almost a tunnel effect over them. The branches grew so densely that they may as well have been completely intertwined. They were beautiful, but also somewhat eerie as they shaded the area as much as they did. It was awe-inspiring—even though they all needed sunlight to thrive, they found a way to live comfortably for who knew how long that tunnel had been there. She knew that it was definitely something that had been there a while, though, or they wouldn't have tangled up so much. Though most of the light was blocked out, she could still see plenty as the sun continued to rise. Soon, the green trees began to fade into golden ones as more and more deciduous trees presented themselves. It was a beautiful mix between the greens and the yellows and reds, and Sophie found herself marveling at the look.

Before long, they parked, and Sophie felt confused. She didn't see anything in front of her. But, Felix must not have made a mistake because he stepped out of the car and opened the door for her to come out as well. He picked up the cooler and the fishing rods and tackle box and waited for her to get situated. As Sophie shut the door, she noticed Felix gazing softly at her. Their eyes met, sending a lightning bolt of energy through her body, and she grinned at him.

"Ready? Let's get going," he said, leading the way. Had his hands not been full, she knew he would have taken hers as they went.

"Where are we?" asked Sophie, looking around. She didn't see or hear any water—how were they supposed to catch fish without water?

"This is my family's favorite fishing place," he said, glancing over at her and then smiling his crooked smile. "Actually, it's my family's fishing place. We own the land."

Sophie was surprised, but that made sense—why else would they have driven along on that private road for so long? "Is there a lake here?"

"A small one," he replied, nodding his head. "It's a great place to go fishing, though. Since we're the only ones who ever fish there, it's always fully stocked."

It sounded perfect to her. And there was something comfortingly private about being able to go fishing on their own without anyone around. They had only been on a few dates, and they had visited each other's homes a few times, but it was nice going on their own private, secret trip where no one else would be with them. It was so comfortably private, and she was thrilled to get that chance.

Before long, the trees gave way to a small lake that was nestled into a clearing. The sun was finally starting to shine on the surface of the water, and it was gorgeous—it was shimmering back the reflection, and as she stared at it, she wondered what it was like to live so far out. There was a small cabin there, next to that lake, with a big window overlooking it. It was gorgeous. Everything was so picturesque that Sophie could hardly believe that she had been protesting going *there* of all places.

Felix laughed. "Like it?" he asked, setting down the supplies.

Sophie nodded her head, at a loss for words at the beauty. From there, they could see the sky above them that had been blocked out all along the private road. She never knew that she could see something so beautiful, and she found herself marveling at it. "It's beautiful," she told him breathlessly.

He smiled at her. "I agree," he murmured, taking her hand. "Come with me." He pulled her along with him, moving toward the cabin.

"Are we going inside?" Sophie asked.

"Yeah, we need to get some chairs. Unless you'd prefer to sit in the mud?" He quirked a brow at her, and she shook her head, grinning.

The inside of the cabin was almost as unbelievable as the lake. It was a warm wooden color inside that gave it the appearance of being brightly cheerful, and she loved it. It had an open concept, with a few rooms at the end of it. However, the living room and kitchen space were open and together, met with dining space in the center and a huge, wooden table with plenty of spaces to sit at. There was even a second floor of what Sophie assumed were more bedrooms upstairs.

"Wow," she breathed as she looked around. "This place is great. Did you come here often as a kid?"

"Yeah, I did," he replied. "I loved being able to enjoy the space. We ran around a lot and got to explore everything. But, lately, we're all too busy. Mom's remarried, and her new husband has no interest in going to the property that she and Dad built together, and Dad died last year. My brothers and sister all married and moved out of the area, so it's mostly just my space now." He was gazing at the ceiling with a faraway look in his eye, and Sophie squeezed his hand in support. That was enough to snap his attention back to what he was doing, and he looked at her. "But, you know what? I love the privacy. The chairs are over here." He gestured to a closet near the front door, and they went over to pick them up. He carried both folding chairs all the way back to the lake, and they got set up.

Before long, they were both sitting right next to each other, fishing poles in hand, staring out at the water together in peaceful silence. Sophie felt a bit bad for him after hearing his story, but she didn't want to tell him that. She wanted to enjoy the rest of their day. Her thumb ran over the smooth reel, feeling the individual lines of nylon, all wound up around it and looking at it. She was unsure of what she should do next.

"So, uh… Felix?" she mumbled, glancing at him almost sheepishly.

"Hmm?" She had snapped him out of whatever reverie he had lost himself in and turned his attention to her. Though he smiled politely at her, she could see the sadness underneath it. She briefly wondered if he really wanted to come out here at all.

She hesitated for a split second.

"What is it, Sophie?" he urged softly.

"So, don't get mad, but…" She looked at the ground.

"Out with it, woman!" he replied with a grin on his face, nudging her playfully. He wasn't actually mad— but he had a penchant for a bit of dramatic flair, and this was one of the times to make use of it. But, his eyes were on her and he was all ears, so she knew that it was time to speak. So, after a long moment of silence, she stared at him and finally opened her mouth.

"How do I know when I have a fish on the line?" She really hoped she wouldn't have one at all—when it was time to put the bait on her hook, she had chosen to do so in a way that was loose, so she didn't have to actually catch anything at all. That was fine with her! If she didn't have to see a fish suffer, she'd be perfectly content.

"You'll feel a tug on the line, and you'll notice that the reel will start to unravel as the fish swims away. But, the first sign is seeing just a little twitch at the tip of the fishing pole. That tells you that there's a fish nibbling at it and that you need to be ready." He looked over at Sophie, almost surprised that she knew so little about how to fish. "Didn't you write that one article on the top ten places to fish near the city?" he asked with a teasing grin.

"Shh! Yeah, but that doesn't mean that I fished at them all! I just went to see them and take a few pictures. I don't fish ever. Like at all. ... So, what do I do when there's a fish on the line?" Sophie looked away from him, sighing and running her hand through her hair. How silly she had been to think that she could get along fishing even for the day!

He chuckled to himself at her protests, and that just embarrassed her more. "Shush!" she squealed, patting his shoulder playfully as she giggled and leaned in for a hug.

Felix kissed her forehead again and smiled at her. "You tug it back—" He paused mid-sentence and stared out at the water. He was unmoving for a moment, and Sophie watched with bated breath. What was he doing? Was that something she had to do too? Would staring out to the water make a fish magically manifest itself onto her hook so she could pull it in for him to deal with? "Oh, I've got something. Watch me." And with that said, he went to work. Sophie had to admit—there was a beautiful craft to his work. His movements were gentle but strong and firm as he began.

The fishing pole twitched, and then the reel started unraveling. She watched as he suddenly held the line tightly to stop allowing it to go any further, and the tip of his rod was flailing about. He was watching the water intently, in his own little world as he worked to drag the fish in. He simply sat there, not moving, with the rod shaking. Sophie wondered if he was supposed to do something or if he needed to wait for something special. But then, as soon as the rod stopped flailing, she noticed that he started reeling again. "I'm waiting for the fish to stop pulling, and when it stops, I pull it back toward me. Every time it stops trying to get away, I pull it back."

It took what seemed like forever—he would pull it back, winding it as much as he could, and then just as suddenly, he'd stop doing anything at all, just holding the reel steady. "It's pulling now," he told her, nodding to the tip of the rod that was shaking. Sophie could see the muscles tightening in his arms as he tried to prevent it from pulling away. It was a clear testament to his strength as he sat there, holding it and stopping any more line from escaping. "It's a big one."

But, then, the fish stopped pulling again, and Felix pulled the pole up, so it pointed toward the sky. The tip of the rod was bent so much that Sophie was convinced that it would snap soon. Then, again, as the fish let up, he started reeling again.

This went on for quite some time, back and forth, and back and forth. Probably five minutes later, Sophie watched in awe as the splashing on the surface of the water grew stronger and stronger as Felix pulled it closer. His arms looked incredibly tense, but the expression on his face was sheer focus. He didn't seem concerned with what he was doing, and he certainly didn't seem intimidated by the weight of the fish.

Soon, it was pulled close enough that Felix could reach in and pull it out. It was surprisingly large for a lake fish—it had to have been almost three feet long, judging by the length as Felix tried desperately to hold it up. It was silvery with mottled skin, and there was a long, pink stripe across the middle. Its gills were flushed with a bright red color.

"What is it?" asked Sophie as she stared. She was uncomfortable as she watched it.

"Rainbow trout," he replied, glancing over to Sophie. "If you're squeamish, I recommend turning away." He waited for a moment for Sophie to turn around and took care of everything that he had to do with the fish. "It'll taste great, though. Rainbow trout tastes a lot like salmon. It's delicious, and if you've never had it fresh out of the water, you've been missing out!"

Sophie felt herself shudder a bit at the thought, but nodded her head. Everything was taken care of within minutes, and he was suddenly cleaning out the fish, preparing it. "Let's enjoy it for lunch, shall we?" asked Felix.

"Sure!" Sophie replied, feigning excitement. She was a bit less than enthusiastic, but she knew she would, at the very least, give it a shot if he wanted her to. She'd just have to be brave about it.

Soon, he had a fire going and was preparing the fish. Sophie couldn't lie—it smelled amazing. He had brought lemon, garlic, and parsley with him and was cooking it in a pocket of aluminum foil over the fire that he had prepared, and the smell was mouthwatering. Maybe it wouldn't be so bad to try it after all. The fish was already gone, and if she didn't, then it would be going to waste.

Sophie was pleasantly surprised when it was time to eat it. She tried a bite and realized that it was amazing. It was so tender and sweet, and the garlic was great at adding to the flavor profile.

"What do you think?" asked Felix.

"It's delicious!" She was so happy he knew how to cook—she felt like a lot of the time, the guys that she had met always thought of cooking as "women's work" or thought that she needed to take care of it all. But, Felix? Not at all—he dove right in to enjoy the whole process. It was almost perfect—he seemed driven to not only find the food but to make it as well. That was certainly impressive, she had to admit as she sat there, enjoying the food. "Thank you!"

They enjoyed the rest of their day together, eating fresh fish, and simply enjoying each other's company. It was fun to talk together. It was great to be able to spend that time just getting to know each other better than they did before. It was so satisfying to find enjoyment in each other's presence. Sophie smiled at Felix. She was amazed at just how much he was coming to enjoy him around, but she couldn't ignore it. He was almost perfect.

Story 3: Winter Paradise

It's wintertime! Sophie is thrilled that she gets to enjoy the moment together with those that she loves. The winter season is filled up with feelings of enjoyment, of warmth, and of celebrating love. Though she doesn't get much snow near her home, her boyfriend Felix has asked her to join her for a trip to a nearby town in the mountains for a date night, and she is thrilled to go.

Sophie's entire house smelled like pumpkin spice. She knew it was what the kids these days were called "basic," but she couldn't help it—it was just so enjoyable. She loved baking everything pumpkin during that time of the year, and she was one of those people who would load up on all the Christmas lights and festivities as soon as November rolled around. She was thrilled to have everything all laid out for her—she wanted to be able to enjoy the moment. She wanted to be able to enjoy the holidays for as long as she could. She loved just how pleasant they were.

That year was no exception. She was currently pulling pumpkin bread out of the oven to set on the counter to cool off to enjoy. It was the fourth round of pumpkin baked goods she had pulled out that week— she had already left pumpkin cookies for all of her neighbors, dropped off pumpkin muffins and scones for Cara and her family for their fancy-schmancy holiday party that Sophie always declined to go to. She loved her friend Cara, but she found that sometimes,

Cara's family was a bit... Smothering, to say the least. She had even left a bunch of muffins for Felix to take to work as well.

She hummed to herself as the smell of pumpkin filled the air. She looked outside her window, unsurprised when she saw the rain falling. It was the Pacific Northwest, after all—rain during the winter months was just a fact of life. But, she was still just as happy to be there—she didn't have to deal with driving through the winter snow, and that was a major plus for her.

As she watched the drizzling rain fall from the sky, her phone buzzed, and she picked it up. It was Felix, calling her, and she quickly answered. "Hey, hon, how are you doing?" she asked him, barely able to contain the grin on her face.

"Great! I was wondering if you're doing anything tonight," he replied. He seemed excited about something.

"Not really, why?" Sophie replied.

"I have something that I want to show you," he replied. Sophie found her smile widening in response. She was excited to see what he had in mind. It had to have been great, whatever it was. After all, whenever he had a surprise, it usually ended up being fantastic.

"Sounds great!" Sophie replied. "What time will you be here?"

"I'll be there at 1. Make sure you pack an overnight bag, okay? We can drop Bella off at my place. I have a dog sitter coming to take care of Koda for the night. She can watch Bella, too." Sophie could hear the excitement practically buzzing on his voice. He couldn't contain it—he just wanted to show her whatever it was that he had in mind, and she found that his own excitement was far too contagious to forget about.

Sophie hung up the phone and ran around, getting ready. She packed a bag and froze. She had never spent the night with Felix before. They had spent plenty of time together, but it was time that was always spent separating when they went their own ways for the night. What was she supposed to wear? What should she bring? She couldn't believe that she would be staying overnight with him!

Before long, she was ready to go, pumpkin bread packed for the road, and everything that Bella needed in another bag to be taken to Felix's home. He wouldn't say no to another baked good... Would he? Of course not, she eventually reasoned with herself— what kind of man refuses baked goods from his girlfriend when they are homemade and fresh? It would be crazy for him to think that.

Not much later, Felix pulled up in a nice SUV, black in color. It was a newer one, and Sophie knew that there was a reason for it. They had to be going into the mountains—he normally drove his more fuel-efficient car around when they were staying in urban areas.

But she didn't mind. Wherever they were going would
be great.

"Hope you're hungry!" Sophie announced as she stuck
Bella into the back seat as Felix helped her load up the
bags. "I made pumpkin bread!"

"More pumpkin? Honey!" Felix feigned exasperation.
"How much weight do you want me to gain? I can't
keep eating this way!" He looked at her with a grin as
he patted on his stomach dramatically, waggling his
eyebrows. "I just can't help myself. Your food is too
good!"

Sophie laughed. "Don't be silly. But, I was making
pumpkin bread. I can't help it. The baked goods
always smell so good! I just have to keep making
them!"

"Well, thanks, hon. I bet it tastes great." He pressed
the button to close the trunk and turned to walk into
the driver's seat as Sophie closed up the back door to
where Bella was sitting and hopped into the passenger
seat. She handed him a generous slice of the pumpkin
bread and watched him with bated breath to see what
he would think about it. She was hopeful that he
would love it as much as she did.

He took the bite, keeping his face stoic and his eyes
straight ahead as he chewed, almost exaggerating the
thoughtfulness as he deliberated the taste of the
bread. "Hmm…" he murmured through another bite.

Sophie could barely stand the anticipation, and he finally nodded his head. "It's passable," he told her with a smirk and a playful wink. She grinned back at him as she wrapped up the bag.

"Well, that's a relief! I was almost afraid that I'd have to bother you to eat it all. Good thing you like it—I have a whole loaf."

"Why so much?" Felix replied.

"Well, everyone knows that the way to a man's heart is through his stomach!" she replied with a sage nod. "I have to keep you around somehow."

Felix laughed at her. "With pumpkin bread?"

"With pumpkin bread!" she affirmed with a grin. "Is it working?"

"Mmm, I think it is." Felix put the car in drive and off they went.

They set off, dropping Bella off and then driving through the mountains to the east, and Sophie wondered where they were going. Every time Sophie asked, he declined to respond seriously. They were clearly going to the eastern half of the state, but Sophie wasn't sure what was over there. There were maybe two cities on the east that were a decent size, but beyond that, everything was small and rural. It was certainly going to be cold, though, and Sophie was relieved that she had packed a whole bunch of warm clothes. She turned the heater on a bit warmer as she looked out the window. The further they drove, the snowier it became.

Soon, they were pulling into a sleepy little town. The sun wasn't set yet, but it was going to soon. They pulled into a parking lot, and Sophie looked around. She wasn't quite sure where they were, but she had to admit it looked great. It was snowy, and all of the buildings that they were around had a Bavarian theme—they were all built with the wooden lattices cross the white buildings. It looked great—kitschy, but nice to look at. And, with all of the snow lining the roads, and the crowds of people all dressed up and bundled in their winter gear, Sophie got the feeling that there was something more to what they were doing.

"*Wilkommen* to Leavenworth*!!*" One person called out to them, his German oddly lacking. Sophie turned to see a man dressed as a Christmas elf—he had a loose green hat and all green clothes. "I hope you're here for a good day!"

Sophie looked around in confusion. She had no idea where they were, but it looked fun anyway. "What are we here for, Felix?" she asked. She was smiling as she looked around, but she was still pretty lost wherever they were. She wanted to find out what the point of the day was and what they were doing in such a small town. It was cool—but it was jam-packed with tourists, and honestly, she was starting to feel a little claustrophobic in the crowds. But, then, Felix squeezed her hand, and she felt a bit better.

"I'll tell you later," he promised, planting a kiss on her hand. "Come over here." They spent the day wandering about the small town. It didn't seem like many people lived there—but a lot of people certainly came from out of town. There were groups of tourists speaking different languages and people who looked around like they had never been there before, much like how Sophie was looking around. There were people who had never seen as much as they could find all around them. And honestly, Sophie is related to them.

There were so many different stores that they were able to dip into. There was a beautiful wine store that they went through, loaded up with all sorts of bottles all around them. There were bottles in just about every color, filled with a different kind of wine for every kind of drinker out there. Felix picked up a bottle for later as they walked through the snow, holding each other's hands as they looked around.

Before long, they found a store that was filled up with all sorts of hats in every kind. There were hats that were silly, serious, and fashionable. There were cute hats and hats so garishly unflattering that Sophie would never so much as put them on her head. However, as she walked around throughout the store, she realized that there was a lot to see. There were all sorts of different styles.

"Hey, Sophie," Felix called to her. Sophie turned around to look at him just in time for him to plop a hat that was shaped like a big cheeseburger on her head. She looked at him oddly but then smiled at him. He laughed back, watching her. But, then, a glance at his phone seemed to remind him about something, and he nodded his head to himself. "Let's go! I want to show you something."

Sophie watched him curiously for a moment before nodding her head and allowing him to take the lead. She had no idea where he was going, but it was probably somewhere fun.

It was just getting dark as they walked outside, and strangely, there was a massive crowd gathering in the park right across the street from all of the cute shops that they were passing. Sophie looked at them all curiously. She didn't have to wait long, however, because suddenly, all of the buildings, in their neat little rows, started turning on a bunch of Christmas lights. They were brightly lit and designed to look like beautiful Christmas houses, lined brightly. Some were golden, others were brightly colored, and others still flashed and shone. They all sparkled and twinkled as they turned on across the entire street. One by one, they shone, and they looked fantastic.

Sophie stared in shock—she wasn't sure what she was expecting, but it was not that. She wore a dumbfounded smile as she looked at it all, soaking it all in. Somewhere down the road, there was Christmas music playing, and she could see lots of people cheering, enjoying the moment. She was happy to be there, and she felt Felix's hand wrap around her waist.

"What do you think about it?" he asked her softly as he looked at her. Despite all of the lights that were shining and the beautiful sights, he was looking right at her.

"It's amazing," she told him.

"So are you," he told her. "I've got one more surprise for you, and we have to head out now. Are you ready?"

She nodded her head, wondering what could possibly one-up what they saw at the moment. She was already plenty surprised, and she wasn't sure just how much more she could take. What could she possibly see that would be better than this? What could possibly be more entrancing than what they were seeing? She wasn't convinced that he could live it up, but he certainly was determined to try. He was certainly interested in impressing her, and she was greatly appreciative of it. She didn't even think that he had to impress her—she liked him plenty the way he was, but he always appreciated the attempts.

So, off they went together, with Felix holding her hand and leading her off. Sophie wasn't sure where they were going, but she knew that wherever it was, it would be good. It didn't take long before they were standing in front of one great, big horse. It had white books and a long, white stripe across its head. It was set up so it could pull a wagon that was brightly lit behind them. The wagon was wrapped up with Christmas lights, too, and it looked almost as stunning as everything else they had seen so far.

Sophie stared at it for a moment. "Isn't that cool?" she said softly. "I bet it'd be great fun to ride on that. I bet they're booked full though! There's no way they're not."

"We are booked full, ma'am. Sorry about that. We often are at this time of the year. You'll need to set up a reservation at least a couple weeks in advance." The driver looked at them apologetically. "I'm waiting for my next ride right now."

Sophie deflated a bit. "Oh, okay," she told him with a sigh. That was disappointing—but understanding. She glanced over to Felix, who was busy fumbling with his phone.

"You're in luck, honey, because this is what I came to show you." He showed the screen to the driver, who glanced, nodded his head and waited. "I bought us tickets to ride the carriage. Would you like to go with me?

Sophie gasped in shock. That was not what she was expecting. "Yes!!" she said happily, clapping her hands. "That sounds fantastic!!" She smiled at him, ready to get going. She could barely contain her joy as she looked at him in admiration. She had never known someone to spend so much time trying to make sure she was that comfortable. No one ever really made her feel like Felix had.

Felix smiled at her as he held out a hand to help her climb up into the carriage. She took his hand and stepped in, scooting along the cushioned bench to allow him space as well, and he quickly filled the seat next to her. He huddled up against her, wrapping his hand around hers and intertwining their fingers with a quick squeeze. Then, he looked down at her with a smile.

Sophie rested her head against his shoulder and took in all of the sights. There was a lot to see—all of the lights all around the city. The graceful gait of the horse in front of the carriage as its powerful legs pulled them along. The people were walking around, making space for the carriage, and looking at Sophie and Felix with smiles on their faces as they looked them.

Sophie felt proud as they went through the city together on the carriage. They looked through the main road, and around the next few blocks as well, gently following the trails. The people naturally made space, and the horse was perfectly content to continue about its way, every step causing jingle bells to ring amidst the clip-clop of its hoof steps. It was chilly as they went along the roads, and they could see their breath in big puffs in front of their faces, but that wasn't enough to remove the smile from either of their faces as they watched around.

They went past several ice sculptures too. There was a whole slew of them, all lined up nicely on the side of the road that had long since been closed off to general traffic. Only foot traffic was allowed, and there were hundreds of people walking along and looking at everything with awestruck faces. They were gorgeous—and she had to admit, she was just as in awe of them as they were. It had to be difficult to carve out such perfect lines. It seemed like it would be so easy to destroy them, but they were able to create such intricate designs as if they were molding clay. Somehow, the designs were there, and as they slowly trotted past them, Sophie looked.

Before they knew it, their entire ride around the town within the carriage was over, and it was time to get off. They thanked the driver, and Felix climbed down first, then offering his hand out to let Sophie down as well. Off they went hand in hand, down the road. "Ready to head in for the night? That wine isn't going to drink itself," Felix told her as she wrapped her arm around his.

Sophie nodded her head in agreement. After a long day of driving, then a few hours wandering around such a beautiful mountain town in the middle of winter, Sophie was ready to tuck n for the day. She wanted to take a nice, warm shower and get away from the chilliness for a while. Off they went, arm and arm. Felix had a plan and a place to take her, and who was she to deny him? So far, everything he had done had been perfect. She had a good reason to believe that the hotel would be just as great, too.

It turned out he had actually rented a nice cabin for the night. It was much smaller than his own cabin but was equally as comfortable. Their night went well, and they settled in happily, enjoying that bottle of wine with each other. Sophie was thrilled. She had been afraid that she was going to be nervous on her date with Felix, but they wound up enjoying every moment. It was peacefully perfect, and she was so glad that they got that chance that winter. She couldn't have imagined a better date for them to enjoy.

Story 4: Caribbean Comforts

Sophie's on vacation! She's gone off with her good friend, Cara, for another summer vacation. This time, she went off on a Caribbean cruise, and one of their stops was a beautiful island where they could scuba dive, and of course, they had to take that option for themselves! It was a wonderful chance for them to have some fun and unwind.

Sophie awoke that fine morning to the sound of waves lapping against the side of the biggest cruise ship she had ever been on. Now, she hadn't been on many cruises in the past, but the few she had been on had never been as extravagant as that one. She woke up slowly and comfortably. On that ship, there was no reason for her to rush awake. There was no work to be done, and Bella was at home being cared for by her neighbor back home. That meant that she didn't have to worry about anything but enjoying her moment there on a bed that was almost unbelievably soft. It was softer than anything she had ever felt before, and she was so happy to be there. She deserved this, she told herself, as she stretched herself out across the bed, spreading her arms widely.

She smiled to herself as she rested there, not quite ready to do anything but sit there. She was enjoying the moment too much and felt like she could have fallen back asleep listening to the sound of the ocean through her window. Cara had, of course, splurged and insisted on the rooms with balconies and windows, so they were able to enjoy the sights, and Sophie had to admit—she was glad that they did. She loved every moment of the gentle sounds of the sea.

That was until she found herself interrupted.

"Hello?" she heard Cara call out, and the door opened up. Whether she wanted to sleep or not, that choice had officially ben taken away. Sophie opened up her eyes, peering over to see Cara peeking her head through their shared door. They had gotten conjoining rooms, as they usually did when they went on vacation together, and Sophie smiled at her.

"Good morning," Sophie said with a lazy wave of her hand as she yawned and stretched out across the bed before pushing herself up to sitting. "So, what's on the agenda today?"

"I'm so glad you asked!" Cara replied, bouncing up and down enthusiastically. She seemed almost uncharacteristically giddy at the moment as Sophie looked at her, and she had to chuckle. "We're going *scuba diving!*" she squealed out with joy. "We're going to be docking soon! Get out of bed so we can get off the ship!"

Sophie had never been scuba diving before, but she was certain that it couldn't be too terribly difficult. After all, she was, at the very least, a great swimmer, and she was confident that she would be just fine if she worked hard enough. All she had to do was make sure that she kept on swimming and that she learned how to use the equipment. It couldn't be terribly difficult. So, without protesting Cara's demands, she pushed herself out of bed and dragged herself to the shower to get ready. At the very least, the fact that they would be in the water all day meant that she didn't have to worry about makeup or to do her hair—she just needed sunscreen and her bikini, with a sundress put on over it. Easy-peasy.

It didn't take long for Sophie to throw everything together, and as soon as she stepped out of her shower, she saw Cara standing outside on the balcony overlooking the ocean. She was watching the water rush past them with a dreamy smile on her face. "Don't you just love cruises?" she asked Sophie with a wide grin. Sophie nodded in response as she looked out the window. She could see land on the horizon and knew that they'd be docking soon.

They made their way all the way downstairs, rushing as quickly as they could. Their cabins were on the top of the ship, and they had to go down a set of stairs to get to the place to check-in for porting. They knew that they would have to go there if they wanted to get off the boat. The tours were already gathering up. Some people were gathered for fishing, jet skis, general tourism, and of course, the one that is there for scuba diving. The various lines and groups were all lined up—they were all ready to go, and Sophie could tell exactly what each and every one of them was going to be doing just by how they were all dressed up. The people going to tour the island they were docking on were mostly wearing khaki shorts and lightly colored shirts. Those who were going to go scuba diving, Sophie found herself realizing they were all wearing swimsuits underneath clothing. Many of the women had themselves wrapped up in sundresses with the bikini straps obviously visible from underneath them.

"There's our group!" Cara announced happily, grabbing Sophie's arm and leading her away. She was thrilled to be there with her, and she made it sure that Sophie knew exactly that. Cara had talked all about how she was ready to go scuba diving the entire time that they were walking to their group. She talked about how she knew what she was doing and how she had been out scuba diving before on several other vacations. She talked about how she got to go diving in all sorts of different reefs, swimming and watching the fish go by. She mentioned getting to go all over the place. She enjoyed being able to watch the fish swim by and actually seeing them dart around her. She talked about seeing the fish like the ones in the movie where they had to go across the ocean.

When it was their turn to go scuba diving, then, they were thrilled. It might not have been Sophie's favorite thing to do, but they had agreed that after their last vacation to Greece, it was Cara's turn to choose out something that they would enjoy together. It was her turn to make concessions and allow Cara that chance to enjoy herself and choose out their main events. So,

Sophie sucked it up and was willing to learn how to scuba dive.

Off they embarked from the cruise ship and Sophie looked around. It was strange being around all of those people that looked completely different. They were clearly happy there—so many people were wandering about with a look of comfort on their faces. Their relaxation was practically palpable as they wandered bout, and Sophie could tell that they were happy there. They were calm and at ease. They looked like they had been able to enjoy their time without worrying so much, and Sophie found herself feeling jealous. She found herself wishing that she could also enjoy the world that they were living in.

Sure, there were tourists everywhere, and wow were there a lot of them. The tourists were obvious in their clothes—they were wearing all sorts of touristy clothes and looking around in just as much awe as Sophie felt as she walked through the area. It wasn't until Cara squeezed her arm happily that Sophie blinked and looked at her friend. "Let's go!" Cara said.

Before long, they were suited up, ready, and heading to their destination for scuba diving. They were all meeting up in a relatively small bungalow on the beach—they were all brought inside with just a bit more space for themselves. They didn't have much room in there, but it was enough for them and a couple of instructors and all of the equipment that they would need for the day. The bungalow was painted a creamy white color with a thatched roof. It was picturesque there where it was, with the cerulean blue ocean behind it and a perfectly clear morning sky.

Each person was given their equipment—a wetsuit and plenty of other equipment. They had masks, goggles, breathing equipment, fins for swimming, gloves, and more. Everything that they could have needed was all lined up right there for them to use, and there was a lineup of tanks for breathing along the back wall. There was a tank for each of them, plus a few extras just in case they were needed.

The guides gave everyone a basic list of instructions, telling them everything that they would need to know and walked them through being able to practice everything they were doing, and before long, they were getting ready to go into the water for the first time. Sophie was thrilled as she carried her tank out to the beach. They were barely a three minute's walk from the shore, and Sophie grinned over at Cara. Sophie was bubbling with excitement, her steps bouncy, and her eyes shining in excitement. Cara was the picture of perfect grace and poise as she walked over, smiling as she made her way over. She somehow managed to make the tank look weightless, and the wetsuit look like it had been made specifically for her. She couldn't quite believe the inner beauty that Cara managed to exude to match the outer, but she had to admit that it was admirable that she could look as beautiful as she did while still having a heart of gold.

Before long, they were in the water, and Sophie found herself glad that they had the wetsuits to keep themselves from being soaked in the water. Yeah, they were in the Caribbean, and yeah, the sun was shining on the water all day long, but they still wanted the protection from the cool water. They were all masked up as they moved deeper and deeper into the water, dipping down underneath it. They sank deeper as they kept going into the water, and soon, they were swimming away from the shore.

Sophie took a deep breath out of habit before dipping her head underneath the water for the first time. The entire surrounding was blue. It was so strange going from above the water to suddenly see everything swimming underneath the water. All she could see was the blueness shimmering all around them. She looked around in awe. She was surprised at what there was around her. The ground underneath them was rocky and bumpy, and at first, Sophie didn't really see anything stand out. It all looked almost monochromatic until she realized that there were fish swimming about. She breathed out a big breath that bubbled around her as she swam, kicking her feet slowly. She made her way down to look at the rocky surface. It was almost reddish-brown in color—they weren't yet at the reef. But, there was still a surprising amount to see. As she got closer to the rocks on the bottom, she realized that they weren't just solid red— they were covered in little plants, organisms, and shells across the bottom. There were tiny crabs crawling about the bottom, one by one, inching their way around them. They were tiny crabs, but they still managed to move around rapidly as Sophie looked at them.

The crabs were maybe the size of her thumb tip as they scuttled around. They were red and white as they crawled around, barely noticeable. As Sophie got closer to them, they'd disappear too, scuttling away to hide in cracks and crevasses. They disappeared almost as quickly as Sophie was able to see them. They were so cute! Sophie leaned in as close as she could to try to see them scuttling around, and realized that she was actually looking at something else. There was a brownish-red sea cucumber there, barely moving. If she looked closely, she could see it undulating in front of her at a slow pace. It was barely moving there for her, but she realized that it was there. She realized she could see it there, shifting about. Where was it going, she wondered as she watched it barely moving.

Sophie felt a tap on her shoulder and when she looked over it, she saw Cara there, staring at her. She pointed further, and Sophie thought she understood—the tour group was going further away. They were going to reach the reef soon, she was pretty sure. They were heading closer to it. Before long, they were there. The reef was gorgeous compared to the reddish-brown ground they had passed up until that point. It was brightly colored and active as they approached. They could see the larger fish swimming about as they got closer. The fish was covered in all sorts of different colors. Red, blue, green, yellow, purple, magenta, and more, all just darted around in the water. There were anemone and coral growing in just about every color imaginable around them. They looked great, and Sophie felt her eyes widen as she looked over everything. The coral reef was alive with all sorts of movement, and everywhere she looked, there were new details to take in. She saw a small school of magenta fish swimming about. They were narrow, and about the size of her hand with a split-back fin. They swam about together slowly, darting from place to place without really doing much. They must have been eating, Sophie told herself, because why else would they circle around the same place over and over without really doing much? She watched as a blue tang fish, deep, vibrant blue with a yellow tail, swam past a coral, dipping behind an anemone.

There was even a small fish that swam about with its tailfin held stiffly behind it, and upon closer look, it was a shark, swimming past. The shark was small— maybe the size of Sophie's arm. Maybe it was a young shark, Sophie found herself thinking as she marveled at the way that the water's rippling waves cast shadows across its silvery skin. It had a little black tip on its dorsal fin on its back, and it moved lithely as it swam across the area. It was slow and deliberate as it moved across, and Sophie thought it was a wonderful thing to see as it moved across. It was wonderful to watch, and Sophie wanted to be able to enjoy the moment as she saw it off, circling lazily around the outside of the reef.

Before long, the shark began to swim away as well, leaving the reef just as silently as it had arrived. The fish seemed to sense that the shark was gone because the entire reef suddenly exploded with life far more vibrant than Sophie had been expecting. She could see the little schools of silvery fish swimming about, and she was convinced that they had to be happy.

Soon, there was a strange-looking fish that poked its head out from behind a piece of the reef. It was bright yellow with a strange looking nose that stretched out. Its tailfin was on a long, narrow stretch of the body that looked almost like a trumpet's bell. The aptly named trumpetfish stopped and looked at Sophie for a moment, or she thought it looked at her, and it stared, simply hovering there in place in the water, unmoving. If it weren't for the gills that slowly opened and closed, she would have doubted that it was okay there. Then, just as quickly as she had seen it for the first time, she watched as it pulled away, disappearing among the various coral reefs that could be seen.

Sophie thought it looked strange, but at the same time, she enjoyed the chance to see a new world. She thought that the different fish were worth traveling so far and learning to scuba dive. There was a small school of red and yellow fish darting about, almost like a fire flickering underneath them. There were yellow fish swimming about as well, and there were some pink ones, too. Sophie watched as there was anemone wiggling along the bottom of the reef, and saw some little shrimp crawling about on the ground as well.

Before long, they were off on their way back to shore, and as they approached, Sophie felt herself feeling a newfound love and respect for the wildlife there. She felt better seeing the different fish learning to live their lives in the wild without much protection at all. They learned to navigate the ocean, not out of choice, but out of necessity, but Sophie still had to respect their commendable spirit and resolve. As she surfaced up for air, she removed the mouthpiece and took a big gulp of air. It was nice to be out in the open air again, and she genuinely appreciated the opportunity.

They made their way back to the bungalow, the entire time, Cara chatting off Sophie's ear. Cara was just as excited as she was and chatted about the little spotted octopus she watched crawling across the reef. They had both seen some interesting things squirming around, and Sophie was so grateful for the chance she had to go see everything during her scuba diving expedition.

The rest of the cruise went well, but little seemed to compare to seeing that entirely new world underneath the water. Sophie thought it was the best thing she had seen in the day. She thought it was fantastic—she thought that she had seen a lot of interesting things that she never thought possible.

Story 5: Girls' Night Out

It's Friday night!! And that means that it's Girls' Night Out! Join Sophie and her best friends as they spend a night enjoying everything that the world around them has to offer. There's a lot to see out there! That fine summer night, they were heading off to a nice restaurant for dinner and wine before heading over to watch a show in the theater. It was a special night for a special occasion!

"You mean, you got the house?" squealed Sophie into the phone.

"Yes!!" exclaimed Cara on the other line. Cara had been house hunting for some time, but most of the homes that her family encouraged her to purchase were far too big, too fancy, or too overwhelming. Cara came from wealth, and her family wanted her to live like it. But, Cara rarely ever wanted to flaunt it. She was quite practical, all things considered. She drove a new Prius because she wanted a higher fuel economy. She went on lavish vacations, but that was because she would rather pay for experiences than things, and she was totally happy to take all of her friends off on her adventures with her. She took an adventure to Greece and to the Caribbean with Sophie in the past year, and now, she was getting ready to settle into what would hopefully be her forever home. Cara and Sophie had gone looking at a wide range of houses, from multi-million dollar properties on the waterfront, to which Cara complained that they were too big or too lavish. *"Why would I need two kitchens when I don't even like to cook?"* she had asked after one of the houses was just too big. They had looked at beautiful mountain properties with fantastic views of the world around them. *"Why would I want to live so far away from everyone?"* she had asked herself.

She had eventually settled down for a nice house that was a bit on the smaller side, but she'd never complain about it. She loved it—it was perfectly graceful without requiring her to walk half a mile to get from point A to point B, and that was something that Cara appreciated. She had chosen a small home near where Sophie lived—the home was beautiful, but nothing like what her family wanted for her. She didn't feel the need to have a house that was so big that it could house ten families when she herself was a single woman without a family. Even then, if she wanted to have children of her own, she wouldn't need a mansion. It would just be more hassle than it was worth to her, and she wasn't interested in dealing with it. She wanted to make sure that she dealt with things differently than she had grown up—there was no need for those great, big halls or rooms the size of a modern apartment. She just wanted to have enough space that she could be comfortable and enjoy herself. Too much space became nothing but a hassle that she didn't want to deal with.

"Congratulations!!" Sophie squealed into the phone happily. "We've gotta celebrate! Where do you want to go?" she asked Cara.

"I've got a plan in mind... Meet me at the restaurant at 6!" Cara's voice was ecstatic, and Sophie could imagine her jumping up and down for joy. Yeah, Cara usually kept it together, but she was also going to be highly excited. Sophie couldn't blame her! Getting a new home was thrilling! When she bought her home, she had been so happy to finally be a homeowner. She was so glad to finally have that space to herself where she could enjoy what she wanted. She loved being able to paint the walls whatever color she wanted—not that she ever did actually paint, but just having the option was enough for her. She loved that if she wanted to paint, she could.

Sophie grinned to herself as she went through the kitchen to make her coffee. It was warm and enjoyable, and Sophie had a great time sipping at it. She wanted to make sure that she would be ready for what would surely be a great party. She was confident that they'd also be inviting a few other friends out to celebrate and knowing that Cara was involved, she was certain that whatever it was would be enjoyable.

By the time that 5:40 rolled around and Sophie needed to leave to meet up, she was wearing a knee-length dress in a nice teal color. It had white flowers printed across it, and the dress itself was flowy—it tucked in at the waist but then flared out in pleats that practically bounced about her when she walked by. She loved that dress. It had spaghetti straps with a nice V-neck cut to it that revealed her defined collarbone and a small white gold pendant that sat right above it. Her makeup was done with a sultry smoky look to it—the eyeliner was accentuated by grey eyeshadows with a hint of green to draw out her brown eyes. She wore deep red lipstick as well, and her face was carefully made up. She had to look great for such an occasion! Her hair was carefully done up so that she was showing off her slender neck, tied up in a loose bun.

When she arrived at the restaurant, Cara was already there, parked in her car. She was watching out for their friends to show up, and one by one, they did. One by one, they gathered. Cara had invited a few people—Sophie was there. They also had a few other close friends. Alyssa, a newlywed, had shown up, her soft features alight with joy for her friend. Their friend, Olivia, walked up as well. Olivia wore a cute black dress. She had a plumper face, and her skin was a warm tan color. Her long, thick black hair hung around her shoulders, and her bangs framed her face perfectly. She wore dark makeup in the cat's eye style with smoky eyeshadow, and her lips were a bright red color. Olivia was a great friend of Cara's—they had both taken the same major in college and spent a lot of time together.

Olivia, Alyssa, Cara, and Sophie all walked toward their favorite restaurant. It was known around town as being a great place to get some wine with a nice seafood dinner, and it was absolutely delicious. The interior of the restaurant was a bit eclectic, but it did its job well. The tables were a nice granite, and the booths had warm, brown and red cushions that were among the most comfortable that they had ever enjoyed. The floor was a bright blue carpet, the color of the deep sea, and there were pendant lights hanging above every single table there. There was a big sculpture of a sperm whale hanging from the ceiling, mouth widely opened as if it were about to take a bite of something. There was a bar on the far end of the restaurant, and the women all looked at each other. Should they go all the way over there to the bar? Or should they choose to sit at a booth?

Cara made a choice for them—a nice booth that overlooked the Puget Sound. They could see a dock of all sorts of lavish, white sailboats that shone in the evening sun, and there were all sorts of people out on the water enjoying it. They could even see kayakers and people on canoes enjoying the summer warmth. They all settled down into the booth with space for everyone. Cara sat next to Sophie, and across from them was Alyssa and Olivia. Their waitress quickly brought them a stack of menus and a bottle of wine along with four wine glasses for everyone to enjoy before dipping away. The waitress seemed to understand the difference between knowing just how much to stick around and when it is a good idea to gracefully dip away. That was a good trait for a waitress—it was good for them to make sure that they were around just enough to be helpful but not enough to disturb the meal.

"So, Cara," Olivia said, placing her head on her hand and leaning in closer. "Tell us about the new place?" Olivia had a smile on her face, ready to hear all of the interesting details of the house, and Sophie grinned back. The house, from what Sophie had seen, was great, but she was also pretty sure that she was the only one that was allowed around it. She looked at Cara, waiting for her to answer.

"The place is marvelous, darling," Cara responded, her own face breaking out into an equally as excited grin as she started to pour the wine. It was chardonnay that smelled delicious as it filled up each of the four glasses in the center of the table. "It's in a small subdivision that's all about privacy. There's nothing but trees all around it, so I don't have to see my neighbors if I don't want to, and it has a beautiful willow tree in the front yard." Sophie tried to imagine Cara doing yardwork and raking up the leaves every autumn, but she was pretty sure that wouldn't be happening. "And inside? It's gorgeous. Very quaint, but in a good way. It's very homey, and that's exactly what I wanted." It was true! The home was not what one would expect a socialite heiress to purchase on her own, but it was beautiful in its own way.

Cara chatted away about her house, describing the beautiful blue-ish grey paint that was on it and the bright, green trees that surrounded it. Even better, however, was the big yard in the back. "It's got plenty of space for children, whenever I'm ready, and I love that about the house," she announced happily with a nod of her head. She smiled back at Sophie, who quickly nodded her head in agreement. It was perfect the way that it was. Of course, Sophie was quite confident that they'd be spending lots of time remodeling the interior. She had already listened to

Cara chat her ear off about how much she wanted to change about the house. She wanted to put in a beautiful hard cherry wood into the home for flooring—she had shown pictures of Brazilian cherry wood that was absolutely gorgeous. She had also been quick to say that she wanted to paint the interior a warm creamy color that would highlight the colors of the wood. The cabinets, she had insisted, would be made of matching wood, and she wanted to get quartz counters and backsplash on the whole kitchen. She loved the idea of having this beautiful look that she could go into and enjoy—modern, but still conventionally comfortable. The appliances had to be replaced too—she wanted them to be nice, stainless steel.

Perhaps Cara's favorite part of the house, however, was the big window overlooking a beautiful yard form the window in the kitchen. The home had such great, big windows that they could see through. The windows made it nice and bright indoors, despite the greyed out surroundings most of the year. Sophie knew that Cara would be happy—she could already see the home is made up into something that would be incredibly cozy to live within. It would be warm and inviting, and it was likely to be filled in rapidly with practical, yet luxurious furniture that would bring the whole look together.

"Are you going to paint the outside?" Alyssa asked, sipping at her wine.

"Maybe—it's such a cute blue now, though!" Cara replied as she took a sip as well.

"But the bigger question," Olivia asked as she grinned at everyone mischievously, "is whether or not you are going to fill that house up with a nice man now that you're moving into your own place." She chuckled, raising her eyebrows suggestively. "It's time to settle down, isn't it? Sophie, does Felix have any brothers? Or cute single friends?"

Sophie gasped, covering her mouth as her eyes widened in faux shock. She giggled behind her hands, looking at Cara to see what her response was, and the response was quite surprising—she saw Cara chuckling, her cheeks turning red. It was hard to tell if it was the wine that was staining them or if she was actually embarrassed.

"You know, I don't need a man!" Cara announced, raising her glass to her friends. "And how could I when I have such great friends?" She tilted her head with a grin. "You all are too kind, you know? You're too great for all of this. But, you know what? You're all more than welcome to come and visit me any time you want. Besides, maybe I'll just be that cat and wine-loving aunt that never actually marries or has kids. I'll look after all of your kids to be the fun one. It'll be great! All the fun and none of the mess or responsibility!" She grinned at them all.

The truth was, Cara was nervous about finding a partner that she would need to set up such an extensive prenup with. She was worried that any man that came near her was really interested in her for the money rather than actually being affectionate toward her, and she didn't want to deal with having to figure out who was who. She wanted to have a good time with people that she could trust, and so far, she couldn't trust any of the ones who had come around. It was too easy to tell when they started having problems accepting that she didn't want to shower them in gifts constantly. She didn't want to pay for them to have a car or cover every single bill when they went out—she wanted them to offer to cover sometimes, too. Not because she believed that it was always the man's job to pay—but because she wanted to believe that she could trust him to also contribute to pay for things that mattered. She wanted to ensure that he would also cover the bills and be willing to jump in and cover things just because she believed that they ought to be a partnership rather than rely on her entirely for everything that she would do. She wanted to make sure that she was not going to be taken advantage of just due to her money.

Really, Sophie couldn't blame her for those feelings-she wasn't wrong to tell others that she wasn't going to deal with the mingling of funds that could potentially cause her all sorts of problems. She squeezed Cara's hand underneath the table in understanding and support, and Cara squeezed hers back. Before the conversation could go any longer, however, the waitress had returned with a platter of food.

Sophie had a delicious shrimp, clam, and mussel pasta placed in front of her. It smelled amazing. There was a nice red tomato sauce that smelled garlicky and slightly spicy alongside the shrimp, scallops, clams, and mussels. The mussels and clams were already opened up for easy eating, and the shrimp were decently sized—each one was about the size of her thumb. There was a nice sprinkling of fresh parsley all cross the top of the pasta as well. She couldn't believe just how amazing it smelled next to the bakery-fresh garlic bread that was placed next to her alongside a generous portion of a caesar salad.

Cara got a delicious looking stuffed lobster dish that was filled up with crab meat as well, and alongside it was a gently steamed vegetable medley. It looked and smelled just as amazing as the seafood pasta. Alyssa ordered a basic shrimp fettuccine that looked as decadent as it smelled, and judging by her total silence after she tried a bite, probably tasted just as good as well. And Olivia ordered a grilled lemon garlic salmon that was practically melting underneath her fork.

Together, they enjoyed their meal, laughing, and chatting about what they thought of Cara's house. It was a great one from what everyone gathered, and they continued to sip at wine throughout the meal. When they were all done, Cara looked around at her friends. "I've got one more announcement to make!" she told them all happily. "We're going to go to the theater next—I got us a private booth to see the new show!"

The women all cheered and piled into their cars. None of them had enough wine to be unable to drive, and they all made their way to the theater, parking, and heading upstairs. The sun was starting to set at that point as they made their way in to hand off their tickets, and they were all ushered up. They were there to see a new musical that was apparently fantastic, according to the phenomenal reviews all over the internet, and they were thrilled to get the chance to not only see it, but to see it in such a good position.

Their seats were perfect—they overlooked everything above them and allowed them to see and hear everything perfectly. It was such a great place to be, and Sophie was beyond thankful for her great friend. Together they enjoyed the show, sipping at more wine from the concessions stand and watching as everyone did their thing. She thought that the show was fantastic—just as good as everyone had said to them. Being able to see it was great.

Before long, the show was over, and they were all on their way to go back to Sophie's home. They were going to spend the night enjoying silly movies with a few more bottles of wine, ice cream, and any other junk that they wanted to enjoy. Girls' night out only happened so often, and when they had a reason to celebrate, they wanted to celebrate big and enjoy every moment of it. They wanted to feel like they were having a good time together—and they were confident that if they were together, they would do just that. It was going to be a perfect night together, celebrating their best friend's newest success.

Story 6: Sophie Swallows the Frog

It's a typical Monday afternoon and as much as Sophie wished that she could do something else, she found herself being resigned to her fate—she had work to do. She had a whole laundry list of errands to run, and she knows that they have to happen sooner rather than later. So, off Sophie goes, ready to take care of everything that she needs to do. Join Sophie as she goes on her way to take care of everything that she needs to do.

With a sigh, Sophie looked out her window. Of course, it was raining. Bella was laying down next to the sliding glass door that led to outside, simply staring at the drizzle as it came down steadily. It continued to drop all around their home, constantly dribbling out of the sky and creating massive puddles. They could hear the pitter-patter of it drumming against their windows. The rain only made that Monday feel even drabber than before, causing Sophie to feel sleepy. It was something about the lack of light—whenever it rained like that, she just wanted to sleep her day away. She wanted to be able to curl up, comfy and warm, in bed, and just let the day pass her by. But, of course, the more that the rain fell, the more she knew that she couldn't do it. No matter how much she wanted to do so, she was stuck. She had to ensure that she was properly adulting as the world told her to.

So, Sophie found that she had no choice but to steal her resolve. She had to tell herself that she was going to go through the day and take care of everything that needed to be done. She was determined to make sure that she got through everything, even if she was miserable. So, she pushed herself up. She forced herself to get up and walk up the stairs. She went straight to her room, showered, and got dressed to get ready to go. "Mondays, am I right?" she muttered to herself as she trudged up the stairs, not really wanting to deal with the day. Mondays sucked, even with her untraditional job and hours. She didn't want to have to deal with everything that she was doing—she just wanted to make sure that she was responsible enough to keep everything stable.

Sophie's parents had not exactly been the best role models on responsibility—she had always been told that she had to do things a certain way, but she had also grown up believing that she didn't really have to do much in terms of making sure that they had stability. Sophie had always moved around a lot—she went from home to home because her parents had never managed to keep things consistent, and Sophie didn't want that life. But, that also meant that she didn't exactly have the best role models or experiences. She had to make sure that she was driven to do better.

Sophie pulled out her phone and looked over her list. She had a whole lot that she needed to take care of that day. She had to pay her mortgage, pay power, stop at the grocery store for food, and run Bella to the vet. It didn't sound like much fun, but she knew that it needed to be done one way or another. She put her clothes on for the day and looked down at the list of things that she had to do. The first order of business was paying those bills—and at the very least, they could be done online. She tapped in the login information and paid both of those in moments. It was nice and simple, but Sophie still had more to do. "Swallow the frog," Sophie told herself quietly as she walked down the stairs, purse over her shoulder.

Though her parents may not have been the best at making sure that she learned how to pay her bills and be responsible, they had taught her one thing: When faced with a laundry list of things that you don't want to do, the best thing to do was simply get it done. Do the worst thing first, her mother would tell her growing up. "Swallow the frog and be done with it. The more you think about it, the worse it will sound, and the more you'll procrastinate. When you stop thinking and just do it, it's easier to tolerate."

Her mother had a point—if she just swallowed the frog, things would be all over, and she'd be done worrying about what she had to do. All she had to do was get it done. She looked at herself in the mirror one last time before walking out the door. She hopped into her car, and off she went. There were a few grocery stores closer to where she lived than the one that she preferred to shop at, but she loved the one that was an extra five minutes away. It was further, but the food was better. It tasted great, and usually, the staff was better suited to helping as well. She knew

that she'd get much better service there than if she
had stuck around at the closing stores.

Off Sophie went, driving down the road, idly tapping
her fingers along the steering wheel. It was a bit easier
to feel energized when she was outside. Though it was
cloudy, the light was brighter, and she felt a bit more
awake. She looked at the other cars that were driving
along as well. They were quickly making their way
through the roads as well. Sophie liked to imagine
where everyone was going as she drove the whole
fifteen minutes to the store that she preferred. She
looked at the first car to her left. It was a purple
minivan-driving by, soaked in the rain. There was a
woman driving it that looked stressed out. The
expression she wore looked like she was ready to just
give up on whatever was going on. She looked down at
the road in front of her, biting her lip like she was
trying not to cry. Sophie felt a pang of sympathy for
the woman.

Was she stressed because the children in the car were
causing problems? As the van passed her, she saw that
the children in the back were unmoving and looking
straight ahead. They looked stressed out as well.
Maybe someone close to them just heard that they
were sick? Or maybe someone passed away? That had
to be it, Sophie told herself—someone must have
passed away, and that was what caused the sadness

that was emanating from the truck so palpably that evens he could feel it.

The car to her right had a much different attitude. The car itself was an older sedan, perhaps 15 or 20 years old, and it had its own fair share of dents and dings in it. It must have been caused by the young driver that was in the car. The kid must have been maybe 16 or 17 in the driver's seat, and he looked a little bit stressed out too, but his source of stress appeared to be the shy young woman sitting in the passenger's seat. It was probably someone heading off on a date, Sophie told herself with a nod and a smile. How cute. She looked so afraid to be there in the car next to him, and she imagined that they were heading to the movie theater for their date.

Sophie turned her attention right back to the road in front of her as she kept on going to the store. Before long, she was there and pulled right into the parking lot. The place was surprisingly empty for the time and she parked near the front of the lot. Yeah, parking in the back was better for the legs, but the constant drizzle convinced her otherwise. She didn't want to deal with it—she just wanted to be there to get what she needed and get out.

She booked it into the store, covering her head with her purse in hopes of avoiding the rain. Immediately, the warm scent of fresh, roasted coffee filled her nose, and she looked over at the café that was there. She smiled and nodded to herself. That sounded perfect. So, in she went to pick up a coffee to enjoy on her shopping trip. If she had to swallow the frog, at least she could do so in style and comfort with something tasty to wash it down with!

Sophie chose a chai latte to sip at, savoring the spiciness that it brought with her, and she loved just how delicious it was. As she went through the store, pushing her cart and enjoying the delicious drink, she found herself feeling a bit better. Perhaps this frog hadn't been as bad as she had thought. She grabbed her ingredients quickly. For the week, she was planning on making a nice garden salad to eat for lunch with some chicken and eggs tossed into it. For breakfasts, she grabbed a bag of bagels to enjoy with some cream cheese. And for dinners, she was going to be making a big batch of spaghetti, and later in the week, a big batch of curry. That would give her plenty to deal with to eat and enjoy as she went through her day. She just had to make sure that she got everything. Along with the ingredients for her meals for the week, she picked up several different fruits to munch on as snacks. Who didn't love having a taste of banana or watermelon sometimes?

With her cart stocked for the week, Sophie turned her attention to the checkout line and made her way over. However, she stopped as she walked past the bakery. There were some delicious cakes there, lined up and ready for someone to pick up. She just had to decide if she wanted one or not. Her eyes fell on a dark chocolate cake that looked decadently sinful. She eyed it for a moment, debating if the cake was something that would be worth the need for extra exercise or not.

She deliberated over it longer and nodded her head to herself, picking it up and putting it in the cart. If she had to run errands, she wanted to treat herself! Besides, adding a treat was a great way that she could also add some pleasantries to the whole nine yards of work she needed to follow.

With her food paid for and loaded into the car, she was off once more. She had to run home to put away all the groceries so she could pick up Bella and take her to the vet. She knew that Bella would be difficult to deal with—she hated the vet and somehow always knew within minutes that they were heading there. She must have memorized the path that was taken, Sophie had told herself the last time she tried. The poor pup had to be kept buckled into a safety harness to make sure that she didn't try to run out the window or climb all over Sophie in a desperate bid to escape. Sophie hated that she'd protest so much, but she still needed her annual checkup, and she needed to get a few booster shots that year, too.

So, upon arriving home, Sophie quickly put everything away and turned to Bella. She smiled at the dog, but somehow, the German shepherd seemed to know that something wasn't quite right. "Want to go for a drive, Bella?" Sophie asked.

The dog perked up at first, but then her ears immediately fell down, and she flopped on the ground. Sophie stared at the dog and sighed. How was she supposed to lug a dog that was more than half her weight outside and into the car? She looked between

Bella and the front door and shrugged her shoulders. She'd just have to force the point. "Time to swallow the frog, Bella. Let's go!" She clipped the leash onto Bella, and the dog looked up at her pleadingly, as if begging her to not take her out to the car. Of course, she did what any responsible pet owner would do, and off they went outside. They walked to the car, and the dog got in, whining softly as she listened. Sophie clipped her leash to the dog harness seatbelt and then sat next to her. "Sorry, girl, but you need this," she whispered as she patted the pup on the head.

They drove off to the vet with ease then. It didn't take them too long to get there, and before she knew it, they were off toward the vet. This time, Sophie didn't have the time to look at what everyone else was doing. She was busy looking at Bella and making sure that the dog didn't try to bound away or push off from the area. She just wanted to make sure that she didn't need to run away from there or do something that would cause them some problems. Sophie patted the dog as they pulled into the vet's parking lot. The rain was still falling, and she knew that they'd have to move quickly, or Bella would take any opportunity that she could to run away and avoid going in. So, Sophie hopped out, clipped her leash onto Bella's harness, and pulled her with her. She just wanted to get the dog in and out as quickly as possible so they would be done. She was determined to make sure that the dog was taken care of and that they'd be able to go, but she wasn't quite sure how to get through it all. So, off Sophie went, tugging Bella inside.

Bella, of course, was the picture of resistance. She pulled back. She resisted. She demanded to be left alone. But, Bella couldn't just go in to get checked out—she had to be taken in as quickly as possible to ensure that they were going to get out of there sooner rather than later. "Please, Bella? Please?? You have to get inside!" She sighed, looking over the dog that was resisting so adamantly. "You have to get inside!"

The dog looked up, and if she could pout, Sophie had no doubt that there would have been a big frown on her face. But, she had no choice—Sophie wasn't to blame here. The blame was that dogs needed to be taken care of, and she couldn't help that. She wanted to keep her best doggy pall healthy, and that meant biting the bullet, swallowing the frog, and bringing the dog indoors.

Bella seemed to sense that Sophie wasn't going to back down. Though she was still clearly hesitant, she whimpered a few times and followed her into the building without pulling back any longer. She stopped trying to get her to stay behind or let her go. As Sophie held the door to the doggy entrance open, Bella slowly went in, tail down between her legs and ears flat on her head.

"Come on, you wimpy dog. It's just the vet!" Sophie patted her head affectionately. "Don't worry so much about it and let's just get it over with already. The sooner we do that, the better. The sooner we head in, the sooner you get to go home and play. Let's go!"

So, in they went, and Sophie checked them into the receptionist. They both sat in the corner near where they were confident that the vet would come out. The vet's office was small—at least on this side. They had two different waiting rooms—one for dogs and one for cats. There were two other people sitting in the waiting room where Sophie and Bella were. Bella immediately dove to hide under the seat while Sophie sat down. There was another person sitting there with her small Chihuahua under her own seat. The dog looked just as miserable as Bella did, and Sophie felt a bit bad. She was sure that dogs hated the vet-- it wasn't like the people could explain to them that they were just there to get checked out or that things would be just fine if they went in without any protesting. They were stuck somewhere getting poked and prodded and didn't understand why. Of course, it had to happen.

There was another dog there too—this one, a puppy, falling asleep in his owner's arms. The puppy was small and red, with pricked ears that were starting to fall down and a look of utter tiredness on its face. The dog was adorable and quite calm.

Before much longer, the vet popped out and asked for Bella to head to the back. So, off, Sophie and Bella went into the back of the room. The appointment, thankfully, didn't take too long. Though Bella always put up a big stink about going to the vet, she also was quite obedient when she was told to do something. Despite the initial protests, she was willing to listen if she had to. She sat there as she was poked, prodded, moved around, and told to stop moving around so much. She was perfectly healthy, declared the vet after a few moments before giving her a quick pat on the head and a treat. Despite their attempts to convince Bella to like the vet and despite the vet's skill at giving her delicious treats every time she showed up, Sophie had never been able to get that sense that the vet was fun instilled in her dog. Maybe it was that the animals could smell that the area was somewhere scary or depressing. Maybe it was that the animals could smell that there were others there that were sick, hurt, or dying. No matter, Sophie was glad that Bella had at least mostly cooperated that day.

With the vet out of the way and feeling thoroughly drained from a day of errands, Sophie loaded Bella into the car. "Time to go, big girl," she told Bella, who eagerly hopped in, ready to get as far away as possible from that area. It was clear that she was ready to leave as soon as possible, and Sophie couldn't really fault her for that. Off they went, heading home. They were ready to eat and spend some time unwinding for the rest of the day.

Story 7: Horseback Trail

Time for an adventure! Felix has asked Sophie to go horseback riding with him! She has never gone before, but she is ready to get going if that is what he wants. She decides that she'll try her hardest. Besides, you gotta try something before you decide that you don't like it. Sophie may be nervous, and she may be a bit afraid of sitting atop a great, big horse, but she is willing to try if that is what it will take.

"I promise, you'll love it," Felix practically purred as he placed a hand on the small of Sophie's back, guiding her toward a building. They were in the middle of a mountain that Sophie had never gone to before. There was a stable there that people could rent horses from, and though Sophie had never tried it before, there was a first time for everything. She was quite confident that she could have a good time if she could get over one thing in particular: Sophie was afraid of heights. The idea of sitting on a horse to ride was almost terrifying to her—she was afraid that she would fall at a moment's notice and that was horrifying for her. She was terrified that she'd be unable to keep herself up on her feet, and she knew that she'd have to cope with that fear when the time came.

Sophie nodded back in response to Felix's comment and wrapped one hand around his arm. It was more to comfort herself than to show her affection, but he appeared to take it differently. He assumed that she was simply cuddly. She hadn't told him her big problem, and instead, she nervously walked alongside him, smiling and nodding whenever he said something so that she didn't upset him. She was afraid that he would be bothered when she told him that she was afraid of horses—but she also had to remind herself that this was *Felix* they were talking about. He was so sweet. There was no way that he'd be upset or angry at her. She just had to be willing to give it a shot at least once, and he'd forgive her. ... Right?

The area smelled of farm, and as they got closer to the small building that hooked onto what looked like a large stable, Sophie noticed that there were some horses that were sitting there, watching them with interested eyes. They knew that people showing up meant that they'd get ridden, and that meant a chance to explore. Sophie, on the other hand, eyed them back uncertainly. She sighed to herself, trying to steel her resolve.

"I hope you're ready, sweetheart," said Felix as he opened the door. The interior of the building was much nicer than she had expected, and they were surrounded by chairs and a nice water fountain as well. It looked nice and quaint indoors, and behind the table, there was a nice-looking woman. She had long, red hair that she had braided into pigtails that hung down over each shoulder. Her kind face was freckled, and her bright green eyes looked at them with interest. She wore a straw hat even indoors and smiled when they made eye contact.

"Welcome to Horse Ridge Acres!" Her voice was energetic and kind at the same time. She seemed like the type that would help them with anything, or the type that would literally give someone the shirt off of her back if she had to. Sophie hoped they wouldn't have to test that theory as she looked shyly up at the woman. "I'm Anne, and I'm here to help. What can I do for you today?" Her voice had a slight southern twang to it as she spoke, and Sophie couldn't help but think back to the stereotypical southern tomboy type who had no qualms with getting dirty when they went to work.

Felix nodded his hed. "Thanks, Anne. I'm Felix, and this is Sophie. We have a two o clock appointment to go riding." He wrapped his arm all the way around Sophie's shoulder and leaned in to kiss her on the cheek.

Anne grinned at them. "I see you right here. Looks like you have Strider and Morning Star today as your horses. Have you ridden before?" Felix nodded in response, but Sophie looked nervous.

"No, ma'am," Sophie replied, looking down.

Both Felix and Anne stared at her. "Never?" asked Felix. "Why didn't you say something about that before we came?"

"I didn't want to let you down," Sophie responded with a shrug of her shoulders. "I figured it couldn't be too hard... Right?"

Felix and Anne exchanged dubious glances, and immediately, Sophie's heart dropped. Did she need to actually do more than just hold onto the reins?

"You know," said Anne, "I've got another horse, Esprit, who should be strong enough to hold both of you up if you want to ride together. He isn't booked this afternoon. But... He is just as spirited as his name implies. Do you think you can handle him?" She looked at Felix. "You've ridden before, right?"

"Yes, many times. I used to keep horses when I was younger, but life happens, times change, and I don't have the time to dedicate to doing so anymore. But, I'm quite confident in my abilities. We'll try him." He squeezed Sophie's hand. At the very least, she had admitted her inability and inexperience prior to getting on the horse, he thought—she could have been seriously hurt trying to ride a horse without the experience.

A few minutes later, they were out in the stables, walking through to the end where the horse named Esprit was kept. When Anne opened the gate to his stall and grabbed his reins to take him out, Sophie

could hear a gruff snort and a stomp on the ground.
She wasn't sure this horse was going to be willing to
take them on their journey either—but they had to try
at the very least.

"Here he is," said Anne, pulling him out. He stared at
her as if debating defying, but followed around.
"You'll have to be careful with him, though," she told
Felix, passing his reins off.

"I've got it," said Felix with a nod. They walked
outside and fitted the horse with a nice double saddle
so Sophie would be able to sit comfortably. Before
long, they were getting ready to mount him. "I'll go
first, and then you come up after," he told Sophie,
climbing up and throwing a leg over the horse. He put
out his hand and pulled Sophie up as well.

Sophie looked down at the ground and felt her head
swimming. She clung to Felix nervously, wrapping his
shirt in her hands and squeezing her eyes shut. Felix
sensed her shifting and instability. "Are you okay?" he
asked, glancing over his shoulder at Sophie. He was
holding the reins firmly and the horse was not yet
moving.

Sophie nodded her head against his back, eyes still
tightly shut. She was nervous and afraid—but she had
no choice. She had to try. She stabled herself and
looked around. The height was intimidating—but she
didn't want to hold them back. She wrapped her

hands around Felix's waist. "Let's go," she said, her voice trembling.

"Are you sure you're okay?" Felix's voice was full of concern.

"Yes," she said in reply, steeling herself a bit more. "I'm okay."

So, they began to ride the horse, slowly at first. Esprit seemed eager to run off, but under Felix's firm guide, he followed instructions relatively obediently. They walked at a slow trot along a trail, and Sophie looked around, trying to focus on anything but the height around them. She looked at just how high up they were and then looked down again. She looked at the fields of flowers that were growing all around them. The fields were almost brownish in areas, but they still had great, big flowers that were sprouting out. There were green leaves in some places, and there were others that were just fields of wheatgrass waving in the winds. There were big yellow flowers that they could see as well that looked great. Sophie could see the great, big sky, too, with massive white clouds billowing around them. There were also trees lining the path.

The longer they rode, the calmer Sophie started to feel. She was trying her hardest not to focus on the height that she had and soon, she began to smile a bit. "I'm sorry I didn't say anything earlier," she told Felix as she watched a few birds flying over their heads. "I should have, but I was afraid that you'd be upset. I mean... We seem so different. I don't want you to feel like I'm not good enough for you."

That was enough to make Felix stop in his tracks. He pulled the reins, and Esprit came to a stop. Felix looked over his shoulder at Sophie. "Honey, of course, you're good enough. You don't have to share all of my likes and dislikes for us to get along. You can be yourself. I don't mind at all. Don't try to change who you are for me. Just be who you are, and I'll be happy."

Sophie nodded her head. "It's just... You love the outdoors, and I..."

"Don't?" finished Felix as Sophie's voice trailed off.

Sophie chuckled and nodded her head weakly. "Yeah," she replied. "I mean, I can have fun, and I really love all of the places that you've taken me, but... I'm also happy spending my time inside with a good book or a movie. And I feel like you might want someone that wants to be a bit more outdoorsy."

Felix shook his head. "Sophie, that's nonsense."

"Are you sure?" Sophie asked him, looking up with big, worried eyes.

"Of course." He nodded his head solemnly as he looked at her. "You're the only one for me, Sophie. You just have to see that and accept it for what it is. If you can do that, we'll be much happier, I think. Just because I want to do something doesn't mean that we have to. Tell me if you don't so we can find something that we both love to do. I want to make sure that you're happy too, and if that means that sometimes, we go to a movie instead of doing what I want to do, that's fine too."

Sophie nodded her head, feeling a bit more comfortable with the whole talk. "Thanks, Felix... The truth is, I'm scared of heights." She finally managed to blurt out what she had been thinking. "So, this whole time, I've been trying not to look at the ground underneath us because it makes me nervous. I'm the kind of person who's passed out looking down. The Space Needle in Seattle? Nope, not gonna do it. I can't look down on the elevator going up!" Sophie laughed nervously. "I just didn't know how I could tell you this all without upsetting you or feeling like a failure. I'm sorry."

Felix shook his head. "Don't apologize so much!" he insisted. "You're fine. How about we head back and go do something that is a bit more enjoyable for both of us, then? I know we passed a few towns on the way here, and I bet we could find a movie theater or a restaurant for dinner instead if you want."

"Smelling like horses?" Sophie laughed. There was definitely a distinct smell when they wandered around

with the horses. Sophie wasn't sure she wanted to
bring that into any restaurants that they went to.

"Definitely!" Felix said with a chuckle to himself. "Or
we could head back to your place, change, and spend a
day in. I'll order takeout sushi or something."

That sounded like much more fun to Sophie than
continuing on that trail with the horse that looked like
he was ready to bolt at any moment in time. She
nodded her head back. "that sounds perfect," she told
him with a hug. Her heart was full as they retreated
back to the barn that they had gone to originally. They
made their way back slowly, but then, something
happened, and Esprit bolted away. Sophie screamed
from her position on top of him, but that seemed to
only embolden the horse even more, and he ran faster.
Sophie squeezed onto Felix's waist and closed her eyes
as tightly as she could before they made their way
back. Felix somehow managed to get him under
control after a moment or two, but Sophie was
terrified.

She rested her head against Felix's head and shook as
they ran by. As the horse finally came to a slower pace
before stopping, she peeked her eyes open, peering
about them. They were back at the barn by some
miracle. Felix laughed. "He probably wants a rider
that will take him for a real run," he told her as he slid
off, holding his hand out for Sophie to climb down as
well. Sophie took his hand, her own, trembling in fear,

and she saw a flash of concern across Felix's face. "It's okay," Felix told her, squeezing her tightly.

So, they went inside, returned the horse, signed the paperwork, and off they went back home. Sophie spent the whole drive staring at the window, shaking slightly as they went. She was willing to chat back here and there when Felix had something to say, but for the most part, she was quiet. Before long, they were back at home, and Sophie couldn't have been happier. She was relieved that they were back and on her own ground. She hugged Felix tightly. "Thank you," she told him as they headed into her house.

Felix smiled and kissed her head. "You still smell like a horse," he replied, squeezing her tightly. "But that's okay because you're still my smelly, Sophie." He laughed and kissed her on the lips. "I'm just glad to be here with you, no matter what we're doing. And you know what? No more horses in the future." He grinned. "I've got friends I can go riding with. We'll stick to less strenuous trips in the future!"

Sophie smiled and nodded her head thankfully. She could live with that. So, she went upstairs to get herself all cleaned up and de-horse-ified, and Felix got to work ordering food for their date that night. As Sophie washed clean, she couldn't help but feel beyond thankful for such as a loving and caring partner to have. She was so happy that he was willing to do that for her. He seemed to really care about her for her, and that was enough.

Guided Meditation 1: Stream of Thoughts

Have you ever felt like your mind was racing within you, and there was nothing you could do about it? Have you ever felt like no matter what you did, you couldn't slow down those thoughts that continued to whirl around within you, flying about and leaving you utterly overwhelmed? Stress... Anxiety... Fear... Sorrow... They can all hold you back if you don't know how to take a step back from them. In this story, you will enjoy a peaceful trip to your own personal stream of thoughts, learning to watch them go by without reaching out to them to interrupt. You will be mastering the art of passive thought observation and eventually letting them go so your stream can run empty, and you can finally drift off to sleep.

Close your eyes, and settle yourself into bed. Get into your most comfortable position as you prepare to be gently guided off to sleep. Take in a great, big, deep breath through your nose. Feel it flowing through your nostrils and down into your lungs. Is it warm? Cold? Just right? What smells does it carry with it? Focus on those smells. Focus on the sensation of your air as it fills up your lungs with air. Your lungs are like balloons, filling up and swelling up until they are full, and there, they give you the energy to live. Graciously thank the air in your lungs for providing you with the oxygen you will need and exhales slowly. Feel the air, warmer now, as it gently whispers over your lips. Does it dry them out? Does it feel gentle? With every breath that you take, you can feel yourself releasing tension and feeling more at peace.

You will breathe in... And out... On counts of five.

You take a deep breath in...

One... Two... Three... Four... Five...

And out...

One... Two... Three... Four... Five...

Your breath helps you to center yourself. You feel yourself relaxing as your breath slowly and gently calms you down. You feel yourself feeling more connected, more at peace, more aware of everything that you do. You are becoming aware of yourself, what you do, and how you feel.

You take a deep breath in...

One... Two... Three... Four... Five...

And out...

One... Two... Three... Four... Five...

Now, focus on the tension in your body. Become aware of any tension you are holding in your head and face. As you breathe in, imagine that you are pushing the tension within your body and down to the center point above your belly button. Let it gather there. Now, feel the tension in your shoulders. Focus on that stress and tension and as you breathe in, feel it moving down to your center. Let it gather there, imagining your tension and stress all becoming balled up in the center. Feel the tension in your arms and hands gathering and flowing in to your center. Feel that center growing with the tension and allow it to build up. Then, take the tension from your chest and upper back, and flow it down toward your center.

Then, go down to your toes and feet, identifying the tension that is there. Push it up, feeling it flowing up your legs, through your pelvis and belly, and noting it as it arrives in the belly. Focus on it as it grows within you and allow it to flow.

Feel all of the tension in your body, all boiled up into one big ball in your core. You've pushed away all of that tension away from yourself, so you can better focus on Allow yourself to feel the weight of that tension and the burden that it has been putting on you. Feel the heaviness on yourself. That tension in your core begins to transform, and you find yourself laying there, with butterflies all over your body, holding you down. You feel them, holding you, pressing against you, and keeping you down. You are trapped by your tension, burdened. It's keeping you awake, lost in your mind...

You take a big, deep breath into your chest. And you breathe out deeply...

As you exhale, all of the butterflies suddenly fly away. They all push off from you suddenly, and they all flutter away, one by one, disappearing into the sky. As they all disappear, you start to feel lighter. You feel more comfortable, more content. One by one, you feel your tensions fade away. You feel more relaxed. You watch each butterfly take away one of your concerns for the day. You watch each butterfly disappear with your stress, and you feel lighter.

You feel like you can move again.

You feel relaxed.

You feel at peace.

Now, in that space where you pulled the tension away, in your center, imagine that peace and calmness flows into you. It is slowly manifesting within your core, filling you with peace, comfort, and the feeling that everything will be okay. You have a big, shining silver ball of peace and relaxation within your core. Breathe in... One... Two... Three... Four... Five... And out... One... Two... Three... Four... Five... As you breathe in, imagine the feeling of relaxation extending throughout your body. Feel it in your head. Breathe in... and out... Feel the relaxation pulsating in your shoulders and arms... Feel it spreading throughout your chest. Feel it spread down to your legs and feet. It fills your whole body, bringing you utter peace and relaxation. Your mind feels incredibly open and ready to go on a peaceful, relaxing adventure. Your body is ready to fall deeper and deeper into your relaxation so you can become more and more relaxed, with the ultimate goal being to help you to fall asleep.

Your mind is at ease, and you continue to breathe deeply. You breathe in… And out… And in… And out… You look all around you, and you realize that you can see something through the darkness. In front of you, a little speck of blue manifests far off in the distance. It scoots closer and closer to you, flowing. It's fluid as it gets closer to you, and you can hear a babbling sound in the distance. You can see it getting closer and closer to you. As it approaches, you realize that it is a little stream. As the stream approaches you, flowing more and more across the vastness of your mind, you can see that there are little specks of something floating across the top. There are hundreds of them, whatever they are, and you move toward them.

Grass starts to sprout around the stream, slowly stretching out from the water and blanketing the vastness of your mind, filling in the dark expanse of nothing that you had found yourself floating within. You see it getting brighter and brighter within yourself. It grows underneath your feet and leaves you feeling treat. You feel happy and content. You feel at peace where you are. You approach the stream. You kneel down and dip your hand into the water. It is coolly refreshing, lightly trickling around your hand. The water flows between your fingers, and you enjoy the feeling. It's not too hot and not too cold—it is pleasantly cool.

You take a deep breath in...

One... Two... Three... Four... Five...

And out...

One... Two... Three... Four... Five...

You watch the water beneath you. You can see that the water is filled up with tiny fish that swim about happily in the short reeds growing underneath it. You can see them darting about, looking for food. They are small and silvery, maybe the length of your knuckle. They look perfectly content as they go about, darting around, and you feel a wave of happiness within yourself. You feel calm. You feel at peace. You feel like you are ready to make some very real progress.

You take a deep breath in...

One... Two... Three... Four... Five...

And out...

One... Two... Three... Four... Five...

Now, you turn your focus to the things floating atop the surface. You see pink flower petals, all lazily drifting in circles as they float down the stream. They are tiny—the size of your pinky nail, and are so powdery pink that they almost look white where they are. They are beautiful, and there seems to be an endless supply of them all. You start to wonder where they are all coming from. You look around, turning to look upstream, and you decide to walk that direction. You pull your hand out of the water and stand up, seeing that the entirety of your surroundings has transformed into something that is full of so much more than you had seen before. You can see that there are trees and grass and hills. There is a sky overhead, a soft, crystal blue color, and you can see great, big, fluffy clouds, slowly floating. They move through the sky lightly, without a care in the world, and you feel at peace too. You feel like all of your negative feelings are fading away. They float away with the clouds.

You take a deep breath in...

One... Two... Three... Four... Five...

And out...

One... Two... Three... Four... Five...

And again, take a deep breath in...

One... Two... Three... Four... Five...

And out...

One... Two... Three... Four... Five...

You turn your attention back to the stream and start to walk along with it. You walk, step by step. The grass is just as lush and thick the further that you go, and you realize that there is no shortage of the little pink petals. You continue walking along, watching them lazily floating. You feel surprisingly calm as you go as if your core were radiating peace out to you so that you could feel as good as possible for yourself. The sound of the water gently babbling over rocks brings you peace, and you can hear a bird singing in the distance somewhere.

You take a deep breath in...

One... Two... Three... Four... Five...

And out...

One... Two... Three... Four... Five...

Soon, you start to smell something softly sweet. It is a beautiful smell, soft and pleasant. You can't quite place your finger on it, but it is a fragrant, floral scent that brings you another wave of peace as you smell it. You notice a small tree just in front of you. The tree is maybe ten feet tall with long, knobby branches that reach out to you. The wood is a deep, inviting brown, and the whole tree appears to be covered entirely in flowers. The flowers are tiny pink blossoms with five petals each. They have little yellow pistils within them, and they smell amazing. The flowers grow in little clusters with each other nearby. They reach out in all directions. You feel uplifted as you see the flowers on the tree. They are cherry blossoms and they smell so inviting as you approach them. They look beautiful, and you want to reach out to touch them all.

You take a deep breath in...

One... Two... Three... Four... Five...

And out...

One... Two... Three... Four... Five...

You take a deep breath in...

One... Two... Three... Four... Five...

And out...

One... Two... Three... Four... Five...

You can't help it—you feel like you have to reach up and touch them, and you do it. You reach out to touch the tree, and you realize that the petals feel just as soft as they look, and they smell twice as good, too. Suddenly, as you touch the petal, it falls down, drifting down, down, down, until it lands atop the stream in front of you. As it lands there in front of you, you are distracted for a moment—you realize that you are thinking about something. Identify that thought that just went through your mind. What was it? Allow yourself to think about it as it goes by until it fades away.

You take a deep breath in...

One... Two... Three... Four... Five...

And out...

One... Two... Three... Four... Five...

Another petal falls down from the tree, drifting just as lazily. You watch it, breathing slowly and deeply as it makes its way, slowly, down to where it needs to be. It works its way down and eventually lands atop the water, making tiny ripples where it lands. You look at the petal as it sits there. Suddenly, you are thinking about the worst part of today. What happened? Allow yourself to think about it. What was so bad about the day? What made it so frustrating or upsetting? What made it easier to deal with? Let yourself continue to ponder the moment, watching as the petal slowly is carried away by the current. Don't fight it as it does— just watch it make its way down into nothingness.

Soon, it disappears out of sight, and as it goes, you allow your thought to go with it. You let go of the thought and the worry that came with it. You let go of feeling like you need to be so frustrated or upset with the moment. You stop caring about the moment—you let go of the anxiety. You are free.

You take a deep breath in...

One... Two... Three... Four... Five...

And out...

One... Two... Three... Four... Five...

You look back up at the tree and see another petal falling down to the surface of the stream, and just as it touches the water, you realize that you are thinking about another thought. You allow the thought to continue its way throughout your mind without interrupting it. You let yourself think about it. You let yourself worry and wonder about it, and once that petal is out of sight, you let it go instead.

The more petals fall in front of you, the easier it becomes to let go entirely as the thoughts flow. Every time you see a petal falling to the surface of the water, the thoughts come and go. Each and every petal is one of the thoughts that go through your mind. Each and every petal is different, and each one will take your mind to different places. Each place that you go to will fill you with different feelings. Some of them will be good, and others may not be. No matter the thought, let it come. Let the thoughts come and acknowledge each and every one as they pass through your mind in the stream. You are looking at the stream of thoughts within your own mind. They are all unique. They are all different. They are all meant to do something different. Even the thoughts that may not be as pleasant still have their own inherent value that matters. Every thought, no matter whether it is positive or negative, maters to you and will help to drive you. Each thought does something on its own. Each thought will allow you to have something more, something better. They are good to acknowledge, and you do not have to shy away from them.

When you find yourself immersed in a negative thought, it is okay to tell yourself to let it go. It is okay to sit back, watch, and allow it to fade away. It is okay to allow it to dissipate over time. It is okay to acknowledge the thought but not react to it. As you watch the petals go by in your own mind, remember that they are just thoughts. They are just passing by on your stream of thought. They are not able to hurt you. They are not able to take control of you or who you are. They are not able to hold you back. They are simply thoughts—they are petals floating atop a river, and they will not harm you.

You take a deep breath in...

One... Two... Three... Four... Five...

And out...

One... Two... Three... Four... Five

You sit there for a while—you can sit there for as long as you would like. You can sit back and enjoy the moments as they pass through. You can sit back and watch as your own trains of thought change over time. They may be positive today as the petals float by, or they may not be, and that's okay. Let the thoughts go. Let the thoughts fade by. Let the thoughts disappear. You will feel more at ease over time. Just let them go.

You find yourself leaning against the trunk of the cherry tree, watching the blossoms and petals float away. It seems like there will be an endless supply of them—and there may very well be. However, you can slow your mind down as well. As the thoughts go, focus on how sleepy you become. Let yourself feel at ease.

Breathe deeply again. In... And out...

Now, focus on your breath again. You are shifting your attention from those thoughts back to your breath. You no longer need to focus on the petals. Now, it is time to relax.

You take a deep breath in...

One... Two... Three... Four... Five...

And out...

One... Two... Three... Four... Five

How does the breath feel? How does the air smell? Can you smell the cherry blossoms? Focus on the scent and embrace it.

You take a deep breath in...

One... Two... Three... Four... Five...

And out...

One... Two... Three... Four... Five

Hear your breath coming in and out of your chest, and do not turn your focus away. Focus on a point in front of you, but do not pay attention to it. Allow your eyes to gently rest there, and listen to your breathing.

You take a deep breath in...

One... Two... Three... Four... Five...

And out...

One... Two... Three... Four... Five

You start to feel calmer as you breathe deeply. The worry that may have set in from the thoughts starts to fade away. You are at peace. You are at ease. You do not want to respond to the world around you any longer.

You take a deep breath in...

One... Two... Three... Four... Five...

And out...

One... Two... Three... Four... Five

You feel the anxiety fade, and you are left instead with a feeling of peace within yourself. You feel yourself feeling at ease at the moment. You feel like you are totally at peace. You feel totally content in the moment. You feel ready to rest. You realize that your entire body is feeling very heavy. It feels ready to sleep. It feels ready to rest and relax without any interruptions.

You take a deep breath in...

One... Two... Three... Four... Five...

And out...

One... Two... Three... Four... Five

Your sleepiness is starting to become entirely overpowering. Your breathing grows slower... Deeper... More peaceful... You are ready to fall asleep.

Repeat these thoughts to yourself:

"I am ready for a restful, peaceful, and wholesome night of sleeping in my bed."

"I am safe where I am, and there is nothing to worry about where we are."

"I am at total peace in my bed at this moment, and there is not anything in this world that could keep me away from the sleep that I am about to enjoy."

Breathe again to yourself.
You take a deep breath in...

One... Two... Three... Four... Five...

And out…

One… Two… Three… Four… Five

Focus on the breath again. How does it feel? You realize that each breath is making you sleepier. You know that you will not be able to fight it any longer. Soon, the petals stop falling into the stream. The water runs clear, perfectly blue as it gently flows past you. The blossoms all fade out of sight.

You take a deep breath in…

One… Two… Three… Four… Five…

And out…

One… Two… Three… Four… Five
With that breath, the tree behind you starts to fade away slowly as well. It is hazy at first but slowly starts to disappear. It starts to become less and less present, and then you realize that you can't rest your back against it anymore. That's okay though—you allow yourself to gently sink back to lay in the softest, plushest grass that you have ever felt. You are comfortable. You are at ease.

You take a deep breath in…

One… Two… Three… Four… Five…

And out…

One... Two... Three... Four... Five.

With that breath, the blue sky starts to fade away.
First, it is a brilliant blue, and then it becomes alight
with the impending sunset. You see the sky turning a
beautiful fiery color as the sunset blazes along the
surface. You see it fading away, little by little. The
fiery blaze of sunset slowly becomes darker and
darker, until finally, the light from the sun is gone.

You take a deep breath in...

One... Two... Three... Four... Five...

And out...

One... Two... Three... Four... Five

In that dark, night sky, you realize that there are
millions upon millions of stars, all lit up around you.
They are brightly shining. They are peacefully
twinkling. There are more than you can possibly count
up there in the sky above you, and you lose yourself in
watching them. Their twinkling is peacefully lulling
you deeper into your own sleep. You feel more and
more tired. You feel ready to fall asleep entirely.

You take a deep breath in...

One... Two... Three... Four... Five...

And out...

One... Two... Three... Four... Five.

With that breath, even the stars start to grow hazy. They start to fade out of sight as you stop focusing your vision on anything around you. You let go of the need to focus. You let go of the need to see. You let go of your need to think.

You take a deep breath in...

One... Two... Three... Four... Five...

And out...

One... Two... Three... Four... Five

The grass beneath you starts to fade away into nothingness as well. You lose your awareness of the sensation of the grass against your back and you let that go. You let go of the need to focus so much upon it. You let it go and get ready to sleep.

You take a deep breath in...

One... Two... Three... Four... Five...

And out...

One... Two... Three... Four... Five.

You take a deep breath in...

One... Two... Three... Four... Five...

And out...

One... Two... Three... Four... Five

You take a deep breath in...

One... Two... Three... Four... Five...

And out...

One... Two... Three... Four... Five

You are ready to sleep now. You continue breathing, softly and quietly, until your mind is gently enveloped by the wonderful cushion of sleep.

Good night. Rest well.

Guided Meditation 2: Hot Air Balloons

Close your eyes, and settle yourself into bed. Get into your most comfortable position as you prepare to be gently guided off to sleep. Take in a great, big, deep breath through your nose. Feel it flowing through your nostrils and down into your lungs. Is it warm? Cold? Just right? What smells does it carry with it? Focus on those smells. Focus on the sensation of your air as it fills up your lungs with air. Your lungs are like balloons, filling up and swelling up until they are full, and there, they give you the energy to live. Graciously thank the air in your lungs for providing you with the oxygen you will need and exhales slowly. Feel the air, warmer now, as it gently whispers over your lips. Does it dry them out? Does it feel gentle? With every breath that you take, you can feel yourself releasing tension and feeling more at peace.

You will breathe in... And out... On counts of five.

You take a deep breath in...

One... Two... Three... Four... Five...

And out...

One... Two... Three... Four... Five...

Your breath helps you to center yourself. You feel yourself relaxing as your breath slowly and gently calms you down. You feel yourself feeling more connected, more at peace, more aware of everything that you do. You are becoming aware of yourself, what you do, and how you feel.

You take a deep breath in…

One… Two… Three… Four… Five…

And out…

One… Two… Three… Four… Five…

Now, focus on the tension in your body. Become aware of any tension you are holding in your head and face. As you breathe in, imagine that you are pushing the tension within your body and down to the center point above your belly button. Let it gather there. Now, feel the tension in your shoulders. Focus on that stress and tension and as you breathe in, feel it moving down to your center. Let it gather there, imagining your tension and stress all becoming balled up in the center. Feel the tension in your arms and hands gathering and flowing into your center. Feel that center growing with the tension and allow it to build up. Then, take the tension from your chest and upper back, and flow it down toward your center.

Then, go down to your toes and feet, identifying the tension that is there. Push it up, feeling it flowing up your legs, through your pelvis and belly, and noting it as it arrives in the belly. Focus on it as it grows within you and allow it to flow.

Feel all of the tension in your body, all boiled up into one big ball in your core. You've pushed away all of that tension away from yourself, so you can better focus on Allow yourself to feel the weight of that tension and the burden that it has been putting on you. Feel the heaviness on yourself. That tension in your core begins to transform, and you find yourself laying there, with butterflies all over your body, holding you down. You feel them, holding you, pressing against you, and keeping you down. You are trapped by your tension, burdened. It's keeping you awake, lost in your mind...

You take a big, deep breath into your chest. And you breathe out deeply...

As you exhale, all of the butterflies suddenly fly away. They all push off from you suddenly, and they all flutter away, one by one, disappearing into the sky. As they all disappear, you start to feel lighter. You feel more comfortable, more content. One by one, you feel your tensions fade away. You feel more relaxed. You watch each butterfly take away one of your concerns for the day. You watch each butterfly disappear with your stress, and you feel lighter.

You feel like you can move again.

You feel relaxed.

You feel at peace.

Now, in that space where you pulled the tension away, in your center, imagine that peace and calmness flows into you. It is slowly manifesting within your core, filling you with peace, comfort, and the feeling that everything will be okay. You have a big, shining silver ball of peace and relaxation within your core. Breathe in... One... Two... Three... Four... Five... And out... One... Two... Three... Four... Five... As you breathe in, imagine the feeling of relaxation extending throughout your body. Feel it in your head. Breathe in... and out... Feel the relaxation pulsating in your shoulders and arms... Feel it spreading throughout your chest. Feel it spread down to your legs and feet. It fills your whole body, bringing you utter peace and relaxation. Your mind feels incredibly open and ready to go on a peaceful, relaxing adventure. Your body is ready to fall deeper and deeper into your relaxation so you can become more and more relaxed.

You can feel your body's tension all fading away, little by little, pushing it further and further from yourself. It dissipates as it emanates away from you, and the more that you sit at rest, the more that you feel like you are able to be comfortable in your spot. The more that you are calm and in control, the more you feel ready to relax.

You can feel yourself growing distant from the tension and worries. You feel yourself drifting away, little by little, moving further and further out and free from those worries and fears that hold you back. You feel like you are almost weightless—and you can be. You can allow yourself to be drifted away to glide through the sky, free from the weight and gravity of your stress that you are experiencing. But, before you do that, you must release the corporeal stressors and worries that you have that are holding you down. You must let go of the pain, the discomfort, and the doubt that will hold you back, and you must do so carefully and willingly.

To achieve that inner peace that you are looking for, you must begin on the ground. If you want to free yourself from the doubt, fear, anxiety, and insomnia, you must first learn to release it all and let it stay away from you. In releasing that fear and anxiety, you can become much more comfortable with yourself. You can begin to drift into comfort, and that comfort as you drift lazily about yourself will help you achieve that relaxation and freedom that you seek for yourself.

You are lighter than you realize. You do not have to be pulled back down to earth, not just now. You can let yourself drift off and fall asleep. All you have to do is surrender yourself to the currents of the air, and you will find yourself floating. Envision yourself for a moment, sitting in a wicker basket. The basket is brown and woven carefully all around you. It is a warm, oak color, and it feels smooth to the touch. You can see that it is carefully and tenderly constructed with each and every fiber right where it should be. The surface of the wood is warm to the touch from the sunlight beating onto it. You focus on the woven basket, looking at the intricacies. Individually, each and every one of those fibers may not be very strong, but when they all come together, they create something powerful—something that can support even your entire weight. You focus on the entire basket now, and you can see that each of the corners of the basket is bracketed and attached to something.

Laying on the ground next to the basket, you realize, is a great, big, limp, deflated hot air balloon. The balloon itself is a vibrant rainbow color. It has geometric patterns of rainbow colors, starting at red, then turning orange, yellow, green, blue, and violet before repeating. The colors ripple across the balloon, brightly creating the entirety of the balloon.

You breathe in... And you see the flame above your head flicker to life. Suddenly, the fire starts to burn, warming the air that funnels into the hot air balloon. With every breath you take, you are going to warm the air that your balloon needs to begin to lift off. You breathe out... And in... And out... And in... And every time that you breathe out, you see the fire continue to burn. It is filling the balloon up, and you can see the great, big, deflated sack slowly start to fill and inflate. You can see it slowly working to create that balloon that will carry you away.

Every breath you take brings you back to that state of inner peace. It helps you to feel like you are right where you belong. It helps you to feel at ease in your skin. Each and every breath fills you up with that utter peace of mind that you were looking for.

Every exhale that you take releases some of your anxiety and stress. Your tension is channeled into the hot air balloon, filling quickly in front of you. It fills rapidly as you breathe. It fills up more and more, and before you know it, the balloon is right over your head. It is not quite filled up enough for you to float away, but you can see it getting close. You can feel the nearly-weightlessness as you sit there inside of the basket, breathing deeply.

And with one final breath, you let go. You release that tension and revel in the moment of utter peace for a moment. And, as you do so, you feel your basket break free from gravity. You feel the gentle bob and sway as your basket slowly starts to pull away from the ground. The flame above you continues to burn brightly, releasing your tension and giving yourself that space that you were looking for. You notice that you begin your ascent into the sky, and every breath brings you just a little bit higher. You are comfortable in the basket and lay down inside of it, looking up at the bright, rainbow-colored balloon that pulls you higher and higher. You allow yourself to watch the rippling of the fabric as the flames warm the air within them. You watch the gentle bobbing of the balloon and feel the swaying yourself as you go.

You cannot see the ground as you look up at the sky, but you are certain that you have floated up quite a ways. You look up at the sky and smile—you are comfortable. You are content where you are. You are enjoying the moment as you continue to breathe, and at the moment, you allow yourself to fall still. You know that if you move too much, you will shake up the basket, and you do not want to do this. You instead gently settle yourself down into your position. You look up at the sky above you, beyond the basket. You look at everything around yourself, and you feel calm.

The sky is a beautiful shade of blue. It is clear and vibrant alongside the rainbow hues of the balloon above you. There are puffy white clouds slowly catching a ride on the current, just like you are. You and the clouds are the same in that moment, allowing the will of the universe to take you wherever it will take you, and you do not feel the need to resist. You do not feel the need to fight the current at all—you exhale and allow yourself to slowly drift about. Your tension is practically nonexistent now as you remain floating in the air.

In the moment, you can feel just how connected you are. You are connected to yourself—your mind, your body, and your spirit are all at ease with each other in that moment. All of you are able to feel entirely comfortable at the moment. You feel at ease. You feel content—true contentment—emanating from within you. You can feel yourself warming up within yourself. You can feel yourself becoming calmer and more relaxed as you sit there. You can find yourself embracing your connection to yourself.

You are connected to the universe as well. Like the clouds above you, you are simply drifting along on air currents that are entirely outside of your control. You are floating among them, not bothering to move at all.

You do not fight them—you simply allow them to continue on as normal. You allow yourself to ride along those currents and see where the world and life take you. the more that you do this, the further that you will get.

You breathe deeply again, and you feel yourself freeing yourself from the anxieties of your day. Work doesn't matter when you are hundreds of feet above the ground. Deadlines don't matter when you are too far away from meeting them anyway. You are too far away from these issues to feel attached or bothered by them. They are as small to you as the winding roads that you would see if you peered over the edge of the basket, seeing them, barely visible on the ground beneath you.

You are at ease as you distance yourself from everything. You grow further away from the worldly complaints and closer to your ability to accept yourself and love yourself. You feel yourself growing attached to yourself and who you are. You feel yourself feeling driven toward embracing the situation that you are in. You feel yourself feeling driven to embrace yourself. You feel content. You feel comfortable and happy. You feel ready to rest and ready to embrace yourself.

You are drifting along now, no longer ascending higher into the sky. Now, you are simply pulled about by the currents. You are at peace where you are. You are content with where you are in the moment, and that is enough. Breathe and enjoy the moment. Allow yourself to revel in the contentedness. Embrace the joy that is starting to spread within you. With each breath in, you draw in more peace and contentment. Your body is completely relaxed at this point—there is no more tension holding you back. You feel happy. You feel ready to rest.

The hot air balloon starts to drift downward. It starts to descent toward the ground. The descent is gentle and smooth. You feel your relaxation spreading as you get closer and closer to the ground. Each breath brings you just a bit closer to the ground. It brings you just a bit closer to being back down to earth.

You take the time to peak over the basket now and the sight is absolutely breathtaking. All around you, you can see gently rolling, green hills. There are patchwork farms on the ground beneath you, and you can see endless sky all around you. In the distance, you can see the silhouette of the mountains looking over everything, faint, but present. You can see that there are people along the ground—cars look as small as beetles crawling across the ground. The roads look like tiny lines scrawled across paper by a child. The houses look like little more than blocks on the ground. You can see that they are there, but they look almost fake.

A little river runs along the ground underneath you as well, snaking gently across the hillsides and winding along the ground. The water reflects back the shining sun in places, and it shimmers as it cuts through the green. The trees look like tiny puffs, hardly bigger than broccoli florets as you remain there in your basket.

You breathe in... And out... and you look down underneath you. You can see the shadow from your balloon lazily dancing about on the ground, flickering and fluttering about as you continue to make your way across the sky. You feel the basket sway underneath you, but you do not mind. You do not mind the fact that the wind tousles through your hair.

Suddenly, you feel the air grow colder. It suddenly embraces you—chilly and washing over you. It isn't unpleasant—just cool, and when you look, you see why: All around you is a giant cloud of mist floating toward you. It is massive as it makes its way toward you, hulking and floating closer and closer. You look at it for a moment, wondering if you should move away from it or embrace it head-on and decide that you will go straight through it without fear. It is cool, but not unpleasant.

The cool cloud leaves a fine layer of moisture on your skin, and you feel the hot air balloon dip a little bit more as the temperature drops. It is not too bad—you accept and embrace it anyway and keep moving forward. You decide to keep on going along without concerns, and you enjoy it. You don't mind letting the atmosphere take you where it will.

You realize that the air is nice and fresh where you are. It is crisp and cool. It is refreshing as you breathe it in through your nose. It smells lightly of rain and of freshness, far from the hustle and bustle of daily life or the pollution that the day may bring with it. It is gently enjoyable to breathe in and the more that you do, the calmer you feel.

You are completely relaxed as you breathe on, beholding the beautiful scene in front of you. You can see for miles and miles, and it is the most breathtaking site that you have ever seen. You are high above the ground and just as high above all of the problems that you are facing. You are high above it all, able to gently drift away, free from everything that would ordinarily bother you. You are free to enjoy the moment. You allow it to bring you calmness and serenity.

You let yourself breathe out any remnants of tension that fill you up inside. You allow it all to fade away, burning as fuel for the hot air balloon. You allow it to continue to burn away as you slowly drift. The balloon continues to descend gently in the air, slowly and carefully moving about until it is finally starting to approach the ground.

You breathe in deeply and breathe out your concerns for the day. Your worries for the future dissipate. Your deadlines and your struggles are all fading away, and you feel at peace. You feel at ease. You feel ready to tackle it all, and all you have to do is choose to keep moving forward. You choose to do so. You choose to embrace it once and for all, and you are glad that you did.

The hot air balloon eventually touches down on the ground, and you are at peace with yourself. You are at peace with the world. You feel free from the struggles of the world around you and free from having to struggle so much in general. All you have to do is breathe.

Description

Bedtime stories aren't just for kids anymore...

Do you find that you struggle to sleep, no matter how hard you try to cope with it? Are you always exhausted even though you know that you shouldn't be? If you find that bedtime is impossible for you to cope with, then this book is for you!

As you read through this book, you will build off of the skills from the previous two books, mastering the concepts of mindfulness so that you can feel far more capable of navigating your own difficult feelings with ease. There is a reason that bedtime stories are so recommended for getting children to sleep; after all— having time to enjoy a story allows your mind to relax and allows you to begin to focus more on the moment. You may be pleasantly surprised and discover that through reading these bedtime stories, you will help your mind relax and ease off to sleep.

In this book, you will continue the use of meditation that has been built in the previous books. Then, you will be provided with several options for bedtime stories. Each story is designed to be a calming slice of life story about the various adventures (and sometimes misadventures) of Sophie Rogers, a young woman that lives in the Pacific Northwest with her German shepherd pal, Bella. Together, and sometimes separately, they get out and enjoy their lives and the stories of her day to day life can help you to relax and soothe yourself into a state in which you will be able to relax. As you read, you should find yourself calming down and preparing for a night of sleep. Each of the options that are provided to you should be fun and engaging without keeping you up at night.

Finally, at the end of the book, you will be given two more traditional mindful meditations that are designed to trigger that state of mindfulness within yourself so you can then begin to relax and enjoy a restful night's sleep. When you utilize these techniques, you can calm yourself down when you need to, allowing yourself to finally fall asleep.

If you're ready to start sleeping better, then you are in the right spot. This book may be able to help you relax enough to fall asleep! As you read, you can expect to see:

- An adventure in which Sophie builds herself a new garden in her yard
- A day trip to go fishing with Sophie's boyfriend
- A horse and carriage date through a beautiful Christmas town
- A scuba diving adventure vacation on a cruise
- Girls' night out to celebrate Sophie's friend's new house purchase
- A day of errands in which Sophie has to force herself to just take care of business and do what needs to be done
- A trip by horseback into the mountains
- Two guided meditations to help you fall asleep with ease

If you're ready to fall asleep, then don't let another day pass you buy. Enjoy these stories and see if sleep is more within your grasp than you realized!

www.ingramcontent.com/pod-product-compliance
Lightning Source LLC
Chambersburg PA
CBHW060946050726
47592CB00003B/1126